EVEN AT 200 MILES PER HOUR, WE MANAGED TO STAY PERFECTLY FOCUSED.

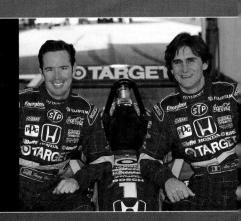

Jake claims his old '64 Mustang GT was so powerful that if he'd jumped on t

But, in his 1999 Mustang GT, all 260 horses are harnessed to a 3.27:1 rear axle th

rebel spirit, but now with advanc

260 pavement-blistering horses.   Standard CD player.   Available All-Speed Tract

celerator hard enough, he could've sheared the rear lugs off. Maybe so. Maybe no.

urs every ounce of power and torque directly into the pavement. Same

epower. So Jake, if you're feeling froggy, go ahead and jump.

New
Mustang GT

ntrol and steamroller Z-rated 245s.   Standard SecuriLock™ passive anti-theft system.

SURGEON GENERAL'S WARNING: Quitting Smoking Now Greatly Reduces Serious Risks to Your Health.

Driver of the Year... Jeff Gordon, right, with canny crew chief Ray Evernham in his corner, gained his second NASCAR Winston Cup in a row, his third in the past four years. The fourth went to Hendrick Motorsports teammate Terry Labonte. Gordon is clearly the man to beat in '99.

On Target... Alex Zanardi, with his mechanical guru Mo Nunn, gained his second PPG Cup in a row in the FedEx Championship, third in a row for Target/Ganassi Racing. After capturing the hearts of CART fans, he's returning to his first love, Formula One.

THE RICH HISTORY OF AMERICA'S ENDURANCE CLASSIC

1962... It all started more than a quarter century ago with Dan Gurney's clever win in the three hour Daytona Continental. His stricken Lotus 19 covered the last two car lengths on battery power.

1966... The first of the true 24 Hour classics spawned a pitched battle between Ford and Ferrari, a rivalry that would endure through the century. Ford Mark IIs swept the field with a 1,2,3 finish. Gurney was a member of the winning driving team.

1967... Ferrari turned the tables, three sleek 330 P4s in front at the finish, piloted by an all-star team of Formula One drivers.

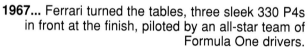

1973... Hurley Haywood won the first of his record five Daytona 24 Hours victories in a Porsche Carrera 1, helping Porsche become the winningest marque in the series.

1988... Jaguar's potent XJR9 broke the Porsche string, again with Formula One talent at the wheel. Porsche fought back to the 1989 win but Jaguar returned in style to a 1,2 finish in 1990.

1991... Porsche again, with its world beating 962. 1992 went to the Nissan R91CP, 1993 to the Toyota Eagle MKIII, the first triumphs for Japanese makes.

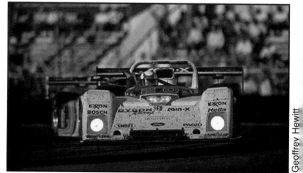

1997... The Ford/Ferrari battles resume in the new era of the World Sports Cars. Rob Dyson's Rain-X Ford R&S, game though wounded, outlasted the Scandia Ferrari 333SP.

Dan Gurney, 1962, 1966.

America's endurance classic attracts the world's elite drivers including winners of the Indianapolis 500, the Daytona 500, and the 24 Hours of LeMans. A sampling of Rolex 24 at Daytona winners follows.

Mario Andretti, Jackie Ickx, 1972.

Hurley Haywood, left, 1973, 1975, 1977, 1979, 1991.
Peter Gregg, right, 1973, 1975, 1976, 1978.

AJ Foyt, 1983, 1985.

Al Holbert, Derek Bell, Al Unser Jr., 1987.

Daytona Racing Archives

Ford and Ferrari again face off in a duel going back to 1966. Ford prevailed in 1997, and a squadron of sleek 12 cylinder Ferrari 333 SPs is out for revenge.

Into the night the battle is waged, with Ford and Ferrari in close contention.

Daytona Racing Archives

Daytona Racing Archives

In the harsh light of day, Gianpiero Moretti's 333 SP prevails, for the first Ferrari victory since 1967.

Luyendyk and Moretti

The jubilant victors roll into victory circle to receive their rewards, the Rolex Cup for car owner Moretti and Rolex watches for him and fellow drivers Mauro Baldi, a Ferrari test pilot, Didier Theys, a Champ Car driver, and Arie Luyendyk, an Indianapolis 500 winner. The crowd pleasing Ford/Ferrari matchup now stands at one all in the current World Sports Car era.

"Nothing reveals more about a race car and its driver than a 24-hour road race." *Hurley Haywood*

Few race car drivers have stood up to the demands of endurance racing as well as Hurley Haywood. With five wins at the *Rolex 24 at Daytona*, three at Le Mans and two at Sebring, he is the world's leading long-distance driver.

Haywood's success is a testament to his patience and discipline as much as to his skill. "In endurance racing," says Hurley, "you're always trying to stay just within the outer limits of your car. Push it too hard, and you'll never finish. Don't push

it hard enough, and you'll never win."

Staying within that zone requires remarkable precision. "A top driver consistently clocks laps within a few tenths of a second," he says. It also requires a rare empathy with the nature and quality of mechanical objects. Hurley Haywood has driven many cars to victory lane, but he has always relied on one special piece of equipment. "I've worn a Rolex for over twenty years," he says, "and it's never let me down."

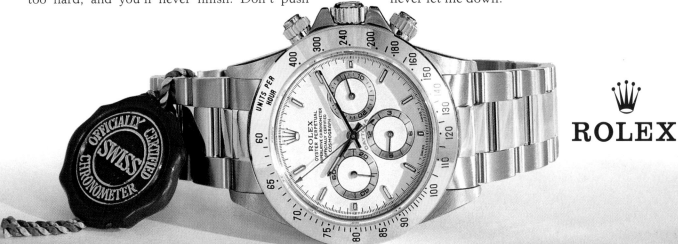

Rolex Oyster Perpetual Daytona Cosmograph in stainless steel and 18kt gold with matching Oysterlock bracelet.
For the name and location of an Official Rolex Jeweler near you, please call 1-800-36ROLEX.
Rolex, ♛, Oyster Perpetual, Daytona and Oysterlock are trademarks.

CONTENTS

CART
FedEx Championship

NASCAR
Winston Cup

Craftsman Truck Series

PPG-Dayton Indy Lights

Pep Boys Indy Racing League

United States Road Racing Championship

Barber Dodge Pro Series

Professional Sports Car Racing

NTB Trans-Am Tour

Published by: Autosport International, Inc.
Publisher: John H. Norwood
Associate Publisher: Barbara Hassler-Steig
Design Director: Robert Steig
Editor: Jonathan Hughes
Front Cover Photography: Richard Dole, Ken Hawking, Nigel Kinrade, Bob Steig, Steve Swope
Back Cover Photography: Steve Swope
Contributing Photographers: Cheryl Day Anderson, Dan Bianchi, Michael C. Brown, Richard Dole,
Ken Hawking, Geoffrey Hewitt, Nigel Kinrade, Bob Steig, Steve Swope, Denis L. Tanney, Sidell Tilghman

Motorsports America, The Men & Machines of American Motorsport, 1998-99
is published by Autosport International, Inc.
37 East 28 Street, Suite 408, New York, NY 10016
© 1999 Autosport International, Inc.

Cheryl Day Anderson

CART'S QUICKEST,
The Marlboro Pole Award Winners

First time pole winners in 1998, Greg Moore and teammate Patrick Carpentier along with Adrian Fernandez, joined the select company of CART drivers who have walked away with some of the more than $2.5 million in Marlboro Pole Awards over the six years of the program. Pole winners get $10,000, plus another $15,000 bonus if they win the event. If they don't, the bonus piles up until somebody does win from the pole. The first and biggest bonus winner of 1998 was Dario Franchitti, who pocketed $340,000 for his Vancouver win after qualifying first. His $370,000 in 1998 awards vaulted him into first place in overall Marlboro Pole winnings. He

topped the '98 list with four poles, Moore collected three, as did Herta, who went on to win at Monterey. Carpentier had two. Jimmy Vasser, Michael Andretti, and Scott Pruett, no newcomers to the ranks, each notched a single pole.

CART's quickest of 1998 lined up at California Speedway's season ending Marlboro 500 as follows: (left to right) Dario Franchitti, Greg Moore, Bryan Herta, Jimmy Vasser, Patrick Carpentier, Michael Andretti, Adrian Fernandez, and Scott Pruett (hidden). Saluting the season's swiftest: CART President Andrew Craig and Marlboro's Ina Broeman.

TOYOTA RACING DEVELOPMENT

LISTEN CAREFULLY AND YOU CAN
HEAR THE SOUND OF OUR ENGINEERS
COMMANDING YOUR RESPECT.

Back to back IMSA GTP championships. Over eighty off-road victories. The
fastest time ever at Pikes Peak. From the drawing board to the cockpit, at TRD
our minds are always racing. Visit www.toyota.com/trd and get up to speed.

TOYOTA | EVERYDAY

CART FEDEX CHAMPIONSHIP SERIES

DRIVERS

By David Phillips

Target-Chip Ganassi Racing had a tough act to follow in CART's 1998 FedEx Championship: They had to defend not one but two titles, seeing as how Alex Zanardi's '97 PPG Cup joined Jimmy Vasser's '96 trophy in the team's Indianapolis display case over the winter. What's more each driver had finished third in his teammate's championship season.

Clearly it was going to take something special to top the past two seasons.

But something special is exactly what Zanardi, Vasser, and Target-Ganassi delivered. The flamboyant Italian scored seven victories to become the first driver since Bobby Rahal to win successive titles and, in the bargain, gave Target-Ganassi the honor of being the first team to win three straight CART titles since Penske Racing turned the trick in '81-'82-'83. Meanwhile, Vasser scored three wins of his own - including a dramatic victory in the Marlboro 500 for the second million dollar payday of his career - to give Target-Ganassi a 1-2 finish in the CART championship.

In his first two CART campaigns, Zanardi got off to slow starts before assuming dominant form. Although he earned the pole at Rio in just his second Champ Car start in '96, he didn't win a race until Portland and ranked a lowly 11th in the points at that stage of the season. He subsequently drove like a man possessed and came within a whisker of pipping Vasser for the title, but '97 was more of the same: He won at Long Beach in April, but didn't begin his championship charge until an epic last-lap

first place drive at Cleveland kicked-off a streak of four wins in five races.

In '98, though, Zanardi hit the ground running and never stopped. Spring wins at Long Beach and Gateway, coupled with seconds at Nazareth and Rio, put him in the drivers seat by June. Then he reeled-off consecutive wins at Detroit, Portland, Cleveland, and Toronto to virtually clinch the title.

A lesser driver might have switched to cruise control, especially with the impending birth of his first child and on-going negotiations with the Williams F1 team occupying his thoughts. But Alex Zanardi is no lesser driver.

He went at it hammer and tongs at 230 mph in the U.S. 500 before finishing third, then banged wheels with Helio Castro-Neves over 12th place at Mid-Ohio, for which he was fined $50,000. Much has been made of Zanardi's technical ability, but what really sets him apart is an indomitable spirit embodied by his spectacular drive at Long Beach (where he came from a lap down to win) and Mid-Ohio's barging match. Whether the contest is for first, 12th, or next to last, Zanardi races to pass the car ahead of him - a point not lost on Frank Williams.

Overshadowed by his teammate, Vasser nevertheless had an excellent season. Concerned by the team's relative lack of pace on the short ovals the past five years, Ganassi & Co. devoted a considerable amount of energy in testing to get a handle on the bullrings. The result was a 1-2 finish at Nazareth headed by Vasser and, a week after Zanardi won at Gateway, Jimmy came home the win-

ner at Milwaukee. In the right place at the wrong time in the closing laps at Michigan, Vasser trailed Greg Moore across the finish line but turned the tables on the Canadian at Fontana to win the Marlboro 500 and the million dollar first prize, bringing his batting average in CART million dollar races to 1,000 (thanks to his win in the inaugural U.S. 500 in '96).

Apart from his trio of wins, the American upped his game by out-qualifying Zanardi a dozen times. Although Zanardi usually had the upper hand on Sunday, the fact that Vasser was stricken by misfortune on several occasions - like a balky full-throttle shift at Cleveland - partially accounted for the yawning points differential between them.

Player's Forsythe Racing and Team KOOL Green performed like championship contenders - for half a season each. Greg Moore was in awesome form at Homestead, leading convincingly until an air jack failed on his first pit stop and he dropped to the back of the field. Undeterred, he scythed through the field, made a fuel-only second pit stop and came within a heartbeat of pipping Michael Andretti at the finish - this on tires with 114 laps on them...

He rebounded from a huge crash to place fourth at Japan's sensational new Twin Ring Motegi, collected more points at Long Beach, moved into the points lead with another podium finish at Nazareth and then joined a select fraternity of Champ Car drivers who have out-dueled Zanardi to win at Rio.

From there, however, it was largely downhill. Although he again made the podium at Gateway, Moore failed to earn points at Milwaukee and finished fifth at Detroit after his Reynard-Mercedes experienced fuel system problems. With Zanardi piling on the pressure, Moore bobbled, precipitating colossal first lap crashes at Portland and Cleveland, and finishing a distant 11th at Toronto. Although Greg scored an electrifying win in the U.S. 500, it would be his final trip to the podium until a game second place in the Fontana lottery.

After joining Moore at Player's Forsythe in the off-season, Patrick Carpentier continued his enigmatic ways in '98. He took his first career pole at Nazareth and followed that performance with another pole at Milwaukee. Although he led handily on the Milwaukee Mile, a coming together with Michael Andretti put-paid to his effort and the eternally upbeat French-Canadian was never a major factor for the remainder of a season highlighted by a seventh place finish at Mid-Ohio.

Like Player's Forsythe, Team KOOL Green had a great half season - in this case, the second half. The intriguing pairing of speedy but inconsistent veteran Paul Tracy with promising sophomore Dario Franchitti boded well for the Indianapolis-based team. But where most expected Tracy to show the way, it was Franchitti who emerged as the dominant force.

Still learning the oval ropes, Franchitti had an inconsistent spring, taking pole at Rio and running well at Motegi, Homestead, and Milwaukee, but crashing at Gateway and suffering an uncompetitive weekend at Nazareth. However, he scored a brilliant second at Long Beach, which would prove to be a harbinger of things to come.

After a steady fourth at Detroit, he gradually emerged as Zanardi's principle challenger, indeed, he became the man to beat. Dario and Team KOOL Green did just that - beat themselves - at Portland and Toronto, where Franchitti took pole and led 76 of the first 79 laps before a braking imbalance on the Reynard-Honda led to a spin. Pole and a first lap crash at Mid-Ohio proved to be the seasonal nadir, for Franchitti and Team KOOL

Green rebounded with a majestic triumph at Road America. A week later he outbattled Andretti in the closing laps at Vancouver and collected a handsome $340,000 in Marlboro Pole Award money in the bargain, as the first pole winner to win a race in more than a year.

Fourth at Laguna Seca, Franchitti was on brilliant form in the inaugural Texaco Grand Prix of Houston, beating Zanardi in conditions ranging from treacherous to appalling. And though the Italian got the better of him at Surfers Paradise, Franchitti went into the Marlboro 500 ensconced in second place in the PPG Cup points race. However, an engine failure while he was running a strong second in the race ultimately dropped him to third in the season's standings but left him as one of the prime pre-season favorites for 1999.

1999 can't come soon enough for Tracy, who suffered a nightmarish '98 season with Team KOOL Green. Unfortunately, it may not start until Motegi in April as he is currently under a one race suspension, to be enforced at the season opener in Homestead.

As for '98, after competitive runs at Motegi and Nazareth were blighted by pit stop gaffes, a series of shunts - some of his doing, others not - led CART to place Tracy on probation after Detroit. He promptly tangled with Michel Jourdain in practice at Portland, leading CART to take the unprecedented step of holding him out of Saturday qualifying and his season never recovered.

After another slow pit stop cost him a good finish in the U.S. 500, he bumped with Tony Kanaan at Vancouver, very nearly punted teammate Franchitti out of the lead at Houston, and then was involved in a public fracas with team owner Barry Green in the pits. The good news was that, by season's end, Tracy's problems were occurring at the front of the field, not the back. The bad news was that an incident with Andretti in Australia prompted CART to exclude him from the first race of '99. To put a perfect coda on the year, he spun out of the lead on a late restart at Fontana, costing himself a chance at a million dollars and

a priceless opportunity at redemption.

Patrick Racing also had a strong season, one highlighted by a couple of wins by Adrian Fernandez. The underrated Fernandez surprised everyone but himself by beating Al Unser Jr. at Twin Ring Motegi and then stayed right in the thick of the chase of Zanardi throughout the summer. He earned his first pole at the U.S. 500 but crashed on race day with horrible consequences as pieces of his car flew into the grandstands, killing three spectators and injuring six more. Thus Fernandez's second win of the season a fortnight later at Mid-Ohio in the Tecate-Quaker State Reynard-Ford was a bittersweet welcome one, and one that cemented his place as one of the emerging stars of the FedEx Championship.

He went on to four more top six finishes, including a fourth place just 1.137 seconds behind winner Jimmy Vasser (and .02 seconds behind Alex Zanardi in third place) at Fontana to secure fourth place in the PPG Cup points race.

Fernandez's teammate Scott Pruett got off to a slow start as various off-season personnel changes on his side of the team took time to gel. But from Portland onwards the Visteon entry normally qualified or finished in the top six, and finished in Fernandez's wheel tracks at Mid-Ohio to complete a Patrick Racing 1-2. A third place at Vancouver and fourth at Fontana pulled him up to sixth in the PPG Cup points race, a personal best and a fitting way to bow out of his association with Patrick Racing and head to his new home at Arciero Wells in 1999.

Many drivers and teams would consider a season in which they won a race and placed seventh in the FedEx Championship a success. But not Michael Andretti and Newman-Haas Racing, especially not in a season in which Andretti led 468 laps - just 31 less than Zanardi - and was outscored seven wins to one and 285 points to 112.

Like Greg Moore and Dario Franchitti, Andretti had a strong half season. Unlike Moore and Franchitti, he failed to take advantage of all but a small percentage of his opportunities. After winning for the second straight season at Homestead, he ran out of fuel at Motegi, crashed while trying to nurse a damaged tire at Long Beach, crashed on a restart at Nazareth, finished second to Zanardi and a quicker pit crew at Gateway, then crashed while trying to pass Carpentier for the lead at Milwaukee.

Six podium finishes were clearly in the offing for the Texaco-Kmart Swift-Ford. Instead, Andretti came out of the first third of the year with just a win and a second place to show for his efforts. And when the season turned to a steady diet of road courses and street circuits, Goodyear proved (again) unable to match Firestone for speed and consistency.

Christian Fittipaldi was not as fast as Andretti early in the year, but his bad luck rivaled anything the Andretti family has ever experienced for he earned just one top ten finish before a welcome third place at Road America. He matched that run with a fine drive at Surfers Paradise and heads into '99 as the most talented driver in CART still looking for his first win.

That dubious distinction, of course, used to belong to Bryan Herta. And through the first three quarters of the season it looked like Herta would carry that albatross around his neck indefinitely. On pole at Portland he led convincingly until his pit crew called him in on an early yellow and he spent the rest of the race fighting his way back to the front. Third on the grid at Mid-Ohio he made a brilliant start to take the lead into turn one only to run afoul of Franchitti; a week later the Shell Reynard-Ford nearly collected teammate/boss Bobby Rahal in a spin at Road America and Herta was lucky to emerge unhurt when Alex Barron slammed into his stationary car.

But it all came right at Laguna Seca where Herta led from pole and was never headed. A late yellow gave arch rival Zanardi one final chance to snatch the victory away - as he had done in such spectacular fashion there in '96 - but Herta was up to the task this time and earned a very popular victory.

That would be the only win of the season for Team Rahal, a fact that was all the more disappointing given the fact that 1998 was "Rahal's Last Ride" and that the three time CART champion was close to victory on a couple of occasions. On the front row at Long Beach he was running strong on race day before a contretemps at the hairpin left the Miller Reynard "beached" and out of contention. Down but not out, he set fastest lap on the way to a 17th place finish. Similarly, he had just taken the lead at Road America and was on track for career win 25 when Herta got it all wrong on the approach to turn five, spun, and clipped Bobby's rear wing. The resulting damage, though minor at first glance, was enough to turn a winning car into an eighth place finisher.

As those races slipped through his fingers, Rahal would have to be content with a popular third place on home turf at Mid-Ohio; that and one of the most distinguished careers in Champ Car history.

Another of CART's most distinguished names - Marlboro Penske Racing - had a terribly disappointing '98 campaign, all the more so given the bright promise the season appeared to hold in store at the outset. Roger Penske had, after a couple of sub-par seasons, pulled out all the stops with the John Travis designed PC27. The car looked the part, from its radical F1 style nose wing treatment to the semi-enveloping cockpit surround for drivers Al Unser Jr. and Andre Ribeiro. But teething problems slowed the car's development and, after Unser's excellent second place at Motegi, results were few and far between. A disastrous weekend on home ground at Nazareth saw Ribeiro crash his PC27 and fail to qualify in the backup, while Unser reverted to last year's PC26 to struggle home 15th.

The PC27 continued to show its promise, especially on the ovals and in Unser's hands - witness a third place at Milwaukee and leading stretches of the U.S. 500 - but the combination of speed and reliability was never quite enough to produce a win. Ribeiro's season went from bad to worse after Nazareth. Seventh place at Vancouver would be his best result, if not his best showing. That came at Detroit where, after going a lap down in the early stages, he matched Zanardi's pace over much of the latter part of the race - confirming the PC27's potential, but raising questions about Andre's consistency.

There was no lack of consistency at Ribeiro's former team - Tasman Motorsports - once talented rookie Tony Kanaan came to grips with the Reynard-Honda Champ Car. After an up and down start to the year, the likable Brazilian got into his stride in August with a string of top ten finishes including back-to-back podiums at Laguna Seca and Houston. But for being rear-ended by Tracy at Vancouver, Kanaan would have had three straight top three finishes. As it was, he came home ninth in the PPG Cup points race, good enough to earn the Jim Trueman Award, emblematic of CART Rookie of the Year.

Kanaan's chief rivals in the rookie competition were former Indy Lights teammate Helio Castro-Neves and F1 refugee JJ Lehto. Neves took over for Patrick Carpentier at Alumax Team Bettenhausen and showed flashes of true brilliance, leading handily at Long Beach and Vancouver before mistakes cost him legitimate chances at victory. At Long Beach he spun while lapping a slower car, while in Vancouver miscalculation on fuel mileage left him stranded on course. The same thing very nearly happened at Milwaukee, where the Alumax Reynard- Mercedes ran out of fuel on the final lap but, happily, had enough momentum to carry Helio across the finish line in second place, just .013 seconds ahead of the rapidly closing Unser.

Lehto had a tough first year in CART, his season made all the more difficult by the growing pains experienced by Hogan Racing in its sophomore Champ Car season. Curiously, the amiable Finn was at his best on the ovals, qualifying his Reynard-Mercedes in fourth at Gateway and eighth at Milwaukee. Mechanical problems denied him good finishes there and he was unable to match that form on the road courses until a strong drive in Australia netted a well-deserved fifth place.

Two of the more disappointing efforts of the year were turned in by Walker and PacWest Racing. A year ago, both had shown ample promise that they would challenge for the '98 title. Gil de Ferran brought the Walker Reynard-Honda to second place in the title race while Mauricio Gugelmin and Mark Blundell helped establish PacWest as the team of the future with four wins. For PacWest, the future will have to wait a little longer, as the '98 season brought nothing but heartache. After a problematic winter testing program with their '98 Reynard-Mercedes, the team opened the year with their '97 cars only to find themselves hopelessly behind on the learning curve when they reverted to '98 equipment. Crashes at Nazareth in the '98 cars put them still further behind and it wasn't until the season finale at Fontana that Gugelmin and Blundell began showing signs of the form that took them to fourth and sixth, respectively, in the '97 championship.

The story was the same, but different at Walker. De Ferran was as quick as ever in the Valvoline Reynard-Honda and was, once again, brutally unlucky not to win at Long Beach when gearbox problems sidelined him after leading 51 laps. That would be a preview of things to come, however, as poor reliability - primarily associated with his development Honda engines - cost him finish after finish. In the stretch from August through October '97, de Ferran collected 58 championship points. During that same period in '98 he garnered all of five points...

Just as the Honda engine played an all too important role in the Walker season, so the Toyota RV8C would be central to the fortunes of Arciero Wells and All American Racers. Arciero Wells experienced a turbulent season on the driver front as Robby Gordon joined Max Papis on the team at Nazareth. He replaced Hiro Matsushita as the Japanese driver and president of Swift Engineering shifted his focus from driving race cars to building them. Later, both Papis and Gordon

would head for greener pastures, with "Mad Max" taking the seat vacated by the retiring Bobby Rahal and the eternally restless Gordon forming his own team.

Amidst the musical seats it would have been easy to lose track of the marked progress made by Arciero Wells and Toyota in '98, most clearly demonstrated by Gordon's superb drive from 24th to seventh at Nazareth and Papis' sensational fifth at water-logged Houston. Although it's true the stop-and-go street circuit and monsoonal conditions played into the hands of Papis and Toyota, the fact that the Italian was regularly knocking on the door of the top ten in qualifying by season's end was a credit both to his inspired driving and tangible progress made by Arciero Wells and Toyota since the dark days of '96. Next year's pairing of Scott Pruett and Indy Lights champion Cristiano da Matta will bear watching.

All American Racers also experienced its share of personnel shuffling, on and off track. Even before the season began Juan Manuel Fangio II announced his retirement, opening a slot for Toyota Atlantic champion Alex Barron alongside P.J. Jones. Later, Swift designer David Bruns parted company with the San Clemente based chassis constructor and moved up I-5 to the AAR shop in Santa Ana to help put the finishing touches on the Gordon Kimball designed Eagle 987 chassis that made its debut at Mid-Ohio in August.

If that seems like a lot to take in in a single season, there's still more. Offered the opportunity to replace the Arciero Wells bound Pruett at Patrick Racing, Jones told AAR boss Dan Gurney in August that he wouldn't be back in '99. Gurney asked Jones to stand down - which he did - and so used the remainder of the year as an extended try out for F1/IRL veteran Vincenzo Sospiri who proved notably ineffective. The good news is that, after an indifferent rookie season, Barron really sunk his teeth into the impressive Castrol Eagle 987 and contrived to lead a chaotic Vancouver race before spinning off under pressure from Andretti. The bad news is that, dwin-

dling sponsorship dollars and support from Toyota mean that the relatively inexperienced Barron (who was racing go-karts full time until '95) will be charged with the daunting task of developing the 987 solo in '99.

At least Barron will have something in common with young Arnd Meier, the determined young German who went at it alone last year with Gerald Davis Racing in developing the Lola T9800 chassis. Last year's T9700 had proven to be a handful.

The '98 Lola appeared to be a reasonable proposition. However, owing to a small budget that precluded much testing and Meier's relative lack of experience, it was difficult to make a definitive assessment of the chassis. However, there appeared to be nothing wrong with the car - or the driver - at Portland when the Davis entry emerged from the first lap confusion in the top ten and stayed there most of the way before slipping to a worthy 12th place finish.

Payton-Coyne Racing tested the T9800 over the course of the season and liked what they saw well enough to go with Lola chassis in '99. Doubtless they hope the switch in chassis will help put them back on the right track after a monumentally disappointing '98 season. A year ago at this time, Payton-Coyne and driver Michel Jourdain Jr. were on the rise, Jourdain having come on like gangbusters after a mid-season switch from Lola to Reynard chassis put him regularly in the rarefied air of the top ten and even saw him bolt into the top three in the opening laps at the Marlboro 500.

Much was expected of Jourdain in '98 but little materialized. A massive crash in testing shattered the young Mexican's confidence and his Herdez Reynard-Ford. That, in concert with a similar incident involving teammate Dennis Vitolo, put Payton-Coyne so far behind the eight ball they never truly recovered.

1998's major story was Target-Ganassi's third championship in a row. With star driver Zanardi gone, Greg Moore and Dario Franchitti nipping at the heels of new leader Jimmy Vasser can they win an unprecedented fourth title in a row?

3 Races
in the CART/FedEx Series
567,668 Fans

175,980
998 Cleveland 3 Day Total

146,135
1998 Detroit 3 Day Total

245,553
1998 Australia 4 Day Total

photo by Alan Vanderkaay

FedEx
CHAMPIONSHIP
SERIES

medic Drug
GRAND PRIX OF CLEVELAND
presented by
★ FIRSTAR

June 27, 1999

TENNECO
Automotive
Grand Prix of Detroit

August 8, 1999

1999
HONDA
INDY
Gold Coast, Australia

October 17, 1999

216-522-1200

IMG *Motorsports Events*

FIREHAWK®
BORN AT INDY.
DRIVEN EVERYWHERE.

FIRESTONE ACCEPTS THE CHALLENGE... AND YOU WIN!

Firestone

THE LESSONS WE LEARN ON RACE DAY ARE IN THE TIRES YOU COUNT ON EVERY DAY.

With a record 50 wins at the Indy 500,® Firestone knows Indy® racing like no other tire company. And if we can develop the kind of quick acceleration, grip and stability required for Indy racing tires, just imagine how well our line of Firehawk® street performance radials will perform for you. Firehawk performance tires are speed rated from S to Z and specifically engineered for crisp handling and legendary performance. We now offer two Firehawk tires with **UNI-T**®, the **U**ltimate **N**etwork of **I**ntelligent **T**ire **T**echnology—

*Firestone Firehawk® SH30™
With UNI-T®
High Performance Street Tire*

the Firehawk SZ50™ and the Firehawk SH30™. The Firehawk SH30 with **UNI-T** is an H-rated high-performance tire designed to deliver outstanding wet performance, especially wet cornering, while still providing excellent dry performance. Stop by your local Firestone retailer and check out the complete Firehawk line today. And congratulations to all Indy teams racing on Firestone Firehawk tires. We wish you much success.

uni·T®
Ultimate Tire Technology

*Race-Winning Firestone Firehawk®
Indy Racing Slick &
Firestone Firehawk SS10™ Street Tire*

Firestone®
America's Tire Since 1900

*Race-Winning Firestone Firehawk®
Indy Racing Rain Tire &
Firestone Firehawk SZ50® With UNI-T®
Ultra-High Performance Street Tire*

Charismatic Champion... **Alex Zanardi**, in three short years on the FedEx Champ Car circuit, captured the Rookie title, two PPG Cups, and the hearts of CART fans. Off to Formula One in '99, he'll be missed.

Cheryl Day Anderson

Dan Bianchi

2 Target/Ganassi's Point Man for '99... **Jimmy Vasser**, with Zanardi gone, takes up the leadership mantle in CART's winningest team of the decade. He was the hottest driver on the late 1998 tour.

Bob Steig

3 Star Caliber... **Dario Franchitti**, in his sophomore year, had a spectacular breakthrough; five poles and three victories. He's a serious contender for top honors in '99.

4 Two Time Winner... **Adrian Fernandez** proved that his lone '96 victory was no fluke, by winning twice in '98 and posting a single pole position for major upward momentum.

Bob Stein

Dan Bianchi

5 Brilliance at Bay... **Greg Moore** led the series after Rio but poor second half performance cost him a serious shot at the championship, despite two victories and four poles. He's one of the favorites for the '99 title.

Dan Bianchi

6 On the Move... **Scott Pruett** scored a pole and eight top five finishes for Pat Patrick's team in 1998, his best year on the circuit, but elected to leave for Arciero-Wells in '99,

Bob Steig

7 Lacking Luck... **Michael Andretti** won the season opening Homestead round, his 37th career victory, added four runner-up finishes and a pole. Otherwise, he had more than his share of misfortune. As usual, a candidate for the title in '99.

8 Winner at Last... **Bryan Herta** finally cracked the win column after years of coming close. Among the year's top pole winners with three, he had the finest performance in his five years on the circuit.

Bob Steig

9 Rookie of the Year... **Tony Kanaan**, made the podium twice in a banner freshman year with Tasman Motorsports.

Bob Steig

10 Saying Goodbye... **Bobby Rahal** completed his "Last Ride" in style, placing in the year's top ten for the 16th year. His best finish was third at his home track, Mid-Ohio.

Dan Bianchi

▮▮ Again Leading Laps... **Al Unser Jr.** passed Mario Andretti to take over fourth place on CART's career lap leader list with 3092. A second and a third place helped improve on his 1997 standing.

Disappointing Year... **Gil de Ferran**, the series runner-up in '97, slipped backwards in the 1998 standings. A pair of third places were his best finishes.

12

Bob Steig

13 Turbulent Tiger... **Paul Tracy**, generally recognized as one of CART's fastest drivers, had several on track encounters with other drivers, which derailed his season.

14 Ending on a High Note... **Christian Fittipaldi** finished off his campaign with a pair of third places after early season struggles and one missed start due to medical reasons.

15 Promise Unfulfilled... **Mauricio Gugelmin** along with PacWest teammate Mark Blundell was expected to be a top contender in 1998, based on their strong 1997 showing. Somehow, the spark was missing.

16 Oval Expert... **Richie Hearn** scored top ten finishes in five of the year's oval events, led 45 laps all on ovals. More is expected in '99.

17 Rapid Rookie... **Helio Castro-Neves** scored the year's highest finish by a rookie, second at Milwaukee, and led more laps than any other rookie, 37, but lost out in the points total to Tony Kanaan.

19 Quick Qualifier... **Patrick Carpentier** set new records in taking the pole at Nazareth and Milwaukee, failed to capitalize on his speed. Crashes in four consecutive races handicapped his point production.

Dan Bianchi

18 Reversal of Form... **Mark Blundell** won three races in 1997, none in '98. Like PacWest teammate Mauricio Gugelmin he had a disappointing season, hopes to turn things around in '99.

20 Formula One Veteran... **J J Lehto** had a difficult entry to CART racing, but posted Hogan Racing's best ever finish, fifth, at season ending Australia event.

Bob Steig

Team KOOL Green: Fireworks in the Fall

Robert Laberge/Allsport

As late as mid-August talent laden Team KOOL Green had not a single victory to show for all their immense driver and engineering skills. The Scotsman with the Italian name, Dario Franchitti; had scored three pole positions and a runner-up slot (Long Beach) but no wins. Nor had Paul Tracy, with 13 wins and 12 poles on his career scorecard, been able to find his way to victory circle in Team KOOL Green livery.

The drought in the win column might have been enough to discourage some teams, but not team leader Barry Green and company.

"Nobody in the team gave up at all," said Franchitti. "Barry just said, 'You're doing everything right. Don't change a thing. Do not do anything different.'" He didn't come up with any crazy advice. He just repeated "Don't change anything. You're doing everything right. It's gonna happen."

"Happen" it did, at Elkhart Lake, where Franchitti and Team KOOL Green parlayed good speed with superb fuel mileage and flawless strategy to lead the final 20 laps on the way to their first win of the season. A fortnight later they followed-up their initial success with a hard-fought victory in the Vancouver Molson Indy with Franchitti passing three-time Vancouver winner Michael Andretti in the closing laps. The win was worth an extra $340,000 to Franchitti as he was the first driver in more than a year to win from pole

position, a feat that earned him a record sum in Marlboro pole award bonus money.

Franchitti went on to add a third win in rain-drenched Houston. A second place at Honda Indy Australia saw him enter the season finale at California Speedway lying second in the PPG Cup points race behind champion-elect Alex Zanardi. But he suffered an engine failure while running second and so slipped to third in the final standings behind Zanardi and Target-Ganassi Racing teammate Jimmy Vasser, the California winner. With Zanardi gone in '99, Franchitti, Vasser, and Player's Forsythe driver Greg Moore stand as the pre-season favorites for the '99 title.

Team KOOL Green's Dario Franchitti and Paul Tracy

Team KOOL Green takes over the Road America victory podium.

Cheryl Day Anderson

With Paul Tracy in the starting lineup you can always count on some sparks. Although he did not enjoy the same degree of success as his teammate, he overcame poor qualifying results to lead four races. As always, his charges through the field were exciting for spectators - and fellow competitors as well.

"We had problems getting the car right for qualifying," said Tracy, "and that always put us behind before we even started the race. Fortunately, by race time we usually had a decent race car and I was able to make up some spots on the track." This is a modest way of saying that once the green flag waved, Tracy took aim at the lead no matter where he started.

Tracy led his first race of the season in Japan, where he climbed from 16th on the grid to the top spot, only to fall back to a fifth place finish. At Milwaukee, Tracy went from his 14th starting position to lead 26 laps, before a slow pit stop dropped him to a seventh place finish. A problem in the pits during the U.S. 500 also cost Tracy, but not before he went from his 15th starting spot to lead the race on nine different occasions. The fans loved it.

With improved qualifying results towards the end of the season, Tracy contended for podium positions at Vancouver, Houston, and Australia. He was leading the CART finale at California Speedway when a heart wrenching spin on a restart less than 10 miles from the finish ended his season.

As the winners of half of the last six races of 1998, Team KOOL Green heads into the '99 season as a favorite to win the FedEx Championship.

"We have an outstanding equipment package (Reynard-Honda-Firestone) and I'm pretty confident that we have a very good handle on what a good (chassis) setup is now. That's apparent from the qualifying of both of our cars in the races toward the end of the season," says Green. (Franchitti, with five, was the year's leading pole producer.) "We've still got a lot of work to do but, interestingly, there are now a lot of teams out there chasing us."

Jamie Squire/Allsport

Two in a row as Dario Franchitti takes over the winner's circle at Vancouver. A third win at Houston made it three out of the season's last six for the dashing Scotsman, launched him as a leading candidate for '99 title honors.

Michael C. Brown

Michael Andretti masters Homestead, again.

FedEx Championship Series Race 1
Marlboro Grand Prix of Miami
Presented by Toyota
Homestead Motorsports Complex
Homestead, FL
March 15, 1998
150 Laps, 1.502 Mile Oval

MICHAEL ANDRETTI MAKES IT TWO IN A ROW AT HOMESTEAD

The track has been reconfigured, but Michael Andretti and his Kmart Texaco Swift Ford still own it. He repeated his 1997 season open-

ing victory in style, holding off pole-sitter Greg Moore in his Player's Indeck Reynard Mercedes-Benz in the closing stages. Their run to the wire came after the day's last restart on lap 121. Moore led the first 36 laps, might have won had an air jack not failed on his first pit stop, dropping him back to the 15th spot. Undaunted, he sliced through the field to become Andretti's closest pursuer at the end. Andretti had no intention of being denied his 37th career victory, the most of any current driver. He prevailed by a scant 0.175 second over the flying Canadian. Defending champion Alex Zanardi, who started sixth in his Target Reynard Honda, provided none of his patented theatrics but scored a solid third place, after

briefly leading twice. Gil de Ferran, in the Valvoline Reynard Honda, had a shot at victory leading twice, and posting the second highest total laps in front, 40, to Andretti's 62. Andretti's teammate Christian Fittipaldi, started fourth, finished fourth. Scott Pruett came from the sixth row at the start to claim the final slot in the top five. Rookie Helio Castro-Neves, who crashed hard in Friday's practice, produced a less severe version of the incident in the race.

The top five points producers following the Marlboro Grand Prix of Miami Presented by Toyota were Michael Andretti, 21, Greg Moore, 17, Alex Zanardi, 14, Christian Fittipaldi, 12, and Scott Pruett, 10 points.

FedEx Championship Series Race 2
Budweiser 500
Twin Ring Motegi
Motegi, Japan
March 28, 1998
201 Laps, 1.549 Mile Oval

ADRIAN FERNANDEZ TRIUMPHS AT TWIN RING MOTEGI

Adrian Fernandez was the day's dominant player in CART's Asian outing at Twin Ring Motegi. From his first row starting slot he led the first 22 laps, the last 30, and enough in between to pile up a total of 102 circuits out in front, more than half the race. At the end he was more than 1.086 seconds ahead of runner-up Al Unser Jr., the Marlboro standard bearer in the Penske Racing camp. It was Unser's best finish since 1996, and a gratifying one, coming as it did, from 15th place on the starting grid. He led twice in the course of the afternoon. Fernandez had to beat more than the other 29 starters to rack up his second career victory and the 21 points that tied him with Greg Moore for the lead in the new season. He fought off a flu bug, using a copious intake of liquids. Moore placed fourth today, just ahead of Paul Tracy whose fifth place finish represented a good effort for Team KOOL Green from a 16th place starting slot. Gil de Ferran failed in his bid to give Honda a victory on its home track but notched a solid third place, to place himself among the year's points leaders. Bobby Rahal made a rare trip into the wall, without serious injury.

Following the Budweiser 500, the top PPG Cup points leaders were Adrian Fernandez, 29, Greg Moore, 29, Michael Andretti, 21, Gil de Ferran, 20, and Al Unser Jr., 16.

Michael C. Brown

FedEx Championship Series Race 3
Toyota Grand Prix of Long Beach
Long Beach, CA
April 5, 1998
105 Laps, 1.574 Mile Road Course

ALEX ZANARDI BACK ON FORM, REPEATS AT TOYOTA GRAND PRIX OF LONG BEACH

Long Beach was the launching pad for Alex Zanardi's championship campaign in 1997. Could history be repeating itself in '98? This time his victory was accomplished "Zanardi style," with a surge from 13th place with the race at the three quarter mark to first with 2.917 seconds in hand at the finish. Once again a prime victim was Bryan Herta, the polesitter and the clear leader with six laps to go. Zanardi passed Herta cleanly, unlike the Laguna Seca bumping incident of 1997. In passing Herta he opened the door for Dario Franchitti who demoted Herta to third place. Admittedly Herta was handicapped by worn tires. Zanardi's handlers at Target-Ganassi Racing had clearly made a better call on tire changes than Herta's managers at Team Rahal. Gil de Ferran again had a strong race going, with a stretch of 51 laps in the lead before bowing out with transmission troubles. Fourth place at the finish went to Adrian Fernandez who assumed the points leadership. Fifth place fell to Rookie Tony Kanaan, a fine placement in his third '98 outing.

After the Toyota Grand Prix of Long Beach the PPG Cup points leaders were Adrian Fernandez, 41, Greg Moore, 37, Alex Zanardi, 34, Dario Franchitti, 25, Michael Andretti, 21, and Gil de Ferran, 21.

FedEx Championship Series Race 4
Bosch Spark Plug Grand Prix
Presented by Toyota
Nazareth Speedway
Nazareth, PA
April 27, 1998
225 Laps, 0.946 Mile Oval

JIMMY VASSER RIDES TARGET/GANASSI STRATEGY TO NAZARETH VICTORY

They hadn't planned it that way, but once committed, Target-Ganassi's two pit stop strategy paid off in victory lane for Jimmy Vasser. Teammate Alex Zanardi who went the conventional three stop route, was a front running force all day and finished second. Until today, short ovals had not been the strong suit for Target-Ganassi. Greg Moore started on the front row alongside his Player's Indeck teammate Patrick Carpentier on the pole. He finished third and took over the series points leadership for the first time in his career, edging out Zanardi by a single point. Carpentier led the first ten laps before losing out to hometown favorite Michael Andretti in the Kmart Texaco car who piled up a string of 102 laps out in front. Running in fourth on lap 123 Andretti had another seige of Andretti luck (mostly bad). A cut tire sent him into the wall. He would certainly have been a major factor in the final countdown. Gil de Ferran matched his '97 fourth place finish while last year's winner Paul Tracy collected fifth place for Team KOOL Green. Bryan Herta was a prime mid-race player, leading 42 laps before fading to eighth.

The PPG Cup point leaders after the Bosch Spark Plug Grand Prix were Greg Moore, 51, Alex Zanardi, 50, Adrian Fernandez, 41, Gil de Ferran, 33, and Jimmy Vasser, 31.

Michael C. Brown

Brazil is beautiful, especially for winner Greg Moore

FedEx Championshp Series Race 5
Rio 400
Emerson Fittipaldi Speedway
at Nelson Piquet International Raceway
Rio de Janeiro, Brazil
May 10, 1998
133 Laps, 1.864 Mile Oval

GREG MOORE'S DARING PASS NIPS ALEX ZANARDI IN RIO

Alex Zanardi is known as the master executor of the daring late race pass enroute to victory. At Rio, he was the victim of just such a maneuver, as Greg Moore went around him on the outside with four laps left. Both of the flying leaders had to get around back marker Arnd Meier at the same time, Moore going high, Zanardi low. Zanardi blamed Meier for his loss. "I came up behind the same back marker who made me lose second place in Miami and for some reason he decided to slow down in the middle of the straightaway. I don't understand how things like that happen when you're competing at this level." Moore understandably had no comment. Third went to a consistent Adrian Fernandez. Interestingly, the three top finishers in the race lined up in the same order in FedEx Championship points after the event. Bryan Herta and Michael Andretti completed the top five. The surprise polesitter was Team KOOL Green's Dario Franchitti whose Reynard Honda succumbed to electrical bothers while he was leading on lap 88. Zanardi led the first 77 laps and the 40 prior to Moore's banzai pass. That left only 17 lead laps to the rest of the field, which included Richie Hearn, out in front for four laps.

After the Rio 500 the top Champ Car points producers were Greg Moore, 71, Alex Zanardi, 67, Adrian Fernandez, 55, Jimmy Vasser, 39, and Bryan Herta with 37 points.

FedEx Championship Series Race 6
Motorola 300
Gateway International Raceway
Madison, IL
May 23, 1998
236 Laps, 1.270 Mile Oval

QUICK PIT WORK HELPS ALEX ZANARDI BEAT MICHAEL ANDRETTI AT GATEWAY

All Michael Andretti had going for him at the two-thirds point in the Motorola 300 was a stretch of 122 laps in front and a lead as big as 12 seconds at one time in the run. It wasn't enough. Target-Ganassi crewmen got pursuer Alex Zanardi out in front of Andretti after they pitted at the same time, following a caution occasioned by Al Unser Jr.'s crash. That was the race. Andretti's best passing thrusts in the final 61 laps were successfully parried by Zanardi, who became the season's first two time winner - and the new series points leader. Greg Moore was on the pole, but was immediately passed by Jimmy Vasser, the other front row occupant at the start. At the end, Moore was third and Vasser fourth. Scott Pruett, in the Visteon Reynard Ford, was the final member of the top five. Once again, Andretti ran a faultless race, had a strong car, but had little luck. Once Zanardi got by there wasn't even enough traffic to afford Andretti the passing opportunities that go with slower cars in front of the leader. Zanardi credited teammate Jimmy Vasser as well as his pit crew for the victory. "We weren't running so great in the morning warm up. Jimmy was. He lent me his 'book' and it worked."

Following the Motorola 300 the FedEx Championship Series points leaders were Alex Zanardi, 87, Greg Moore, 85, Adrian Fernandez, 55, Jimmy Vasser, 51, and Michael Andretti with 49 points.

Michael C. Brown

Milwaukee Master... Jimmy Vasser is flanked by Rookie Helio Castro-Neves and Al Unser Jr. on the dais.

FedEx Championship Series Race 7
Miller Lite 200
The Milwaukee Mile
West Allis, WI
May 31, 1998
200 Laps, 1.032 Mile Oval

MASTER OF THE ONE MILE OVALS, JIMMY VASSER SCORES AT MILWAUKEE

Jimmy Vasser joined teammate Alex Zanardi as the year's only two time winners by taking the Miller Lite 200. Vasser set a race average speed record of 131.349 mph at the venerable oval. He finished with a handsome 7.673 second cushion over surprise runner-up, Rookie Helio Castro-Neves of Bettenhausen Motorsports, matching the team's best finish of last year. Once again, the Target-Ganassi team got good marks from Vasser, who credited his ultra fast last pit stop with giving him an edge for the last 75 laps, which he ran off largely unchallenged. "It was a great pit stop. But then we've been working as a team to master the black art of one mile ovals. The car changes so much from the beginning of a fuel run to the end. We were consistent and that's the way you usually win on one mile ovals." Castro-Neves was ecstatic about his recovery of form after a bruising practice accident in the season opener. Unser Jr.'s podium finish hopefully signals better things to come for the Marlboro Penske forces. Dario Franchitti and Bobby Rahal completed the top five. Pole-sitter Patrick Carpentier led the first 16 laps until a tangle with Michael Andretti, a five time winner here, took them both out.

The leading PPG Cup points producers after the Miller Lite 200 were Alex Zanardi, 92, Greg Moore, 85, Jimmy Vasser, 72, Adrian Fernandez, 59, and Michael Andretti, 49.

FedEx Championship Series Race 8
ITT Automotive Detroit Grand Prix
The Raceway on Belle Isle
Detroit, MI
June 7, 1998
72 Laps, 2.346 Mile Road Course

ZANARDI DOMINATES IN DETROIT

There were only two race leaders in a record setting ITT Automotive Detroit Grand Prix; pole-sitter Greg Moore, the 1997 winner, and Alex Zanardi, who started alongside Moore on the front row. Moore set a fast pace and led the first 22 laps before pitting under green. Zanardi didn't even have to pass Moore on the track. He stayed out two laps longer, and benefitted from a fast first pit stop. Once in the lead he stayed there, winning by more than six seconds, while setting a new race record average speed of 100.052 mph. Moore slipped to fifth place at the end but retained his hold on second place in the points standings. Adrian Fernandez started third, ended up with runner-up honors ahead of Gil de Ferran. Zanardi was blessed with good fortune after he grazed the wall in the morning warmup. The only repair required was a wheel replacement. "This morning for the warmup we made a lot of changes. On my second flying lap I ran out of talent and hit the wall. We kept the setup anyway and it turned out to be the right call." Team KOOL Green's Dario Franchitti placed fourth for the second race in a row. On the tire front, Zanardi's win made it seven in a row for Firestone and 18 out of the last 19.

After the ITT Automotive Detroit Grand Prix the PPG Cup points leaders were Alex Zanardi, 113, Greg Moore, 96, Jimmy Vasser, 80, Adrian Fernandez, 75, Gil de Ferran, 55.

FedEx Championship Series Race 9
Budweiser/G.I. Joe's 200
Presented by Texaco-Havoline
Portland International Raceway
Portland, OR
June 21, 1998
98 Laps, 1.967 Mile Road Course

ALEX ZANARDI
PREVAILS AT PORTLAND

Alex Zanardi's decisive win at Portland, his second in a row made it four in a row for Target-Ganassi Racing. The team is aiming for a one-two finish in the FedEx Championship in 1998, after two successive years with a one-three record, in itself a worthy accomplishment. Greg Moore, the current holder of second place in the title chase, did his cause no good by initiating a major first lap tangle. Jimmy Vasser, the other half of the Target-Ganassi driving team, holds down third place in the standings, despite today's eighth place finish. Scott Pruett, though never in the lead, scored a fine second place. Bryan Herta, again the polesitter, was unable to capitalize on his speed ending up third, after running off 20 laps out in front. On hindsight he was handi-capped by an early, out-of-phase pit stop. "The pit stop strategy was the story of the race. We decided an early stop was the way to go, but I don't think it worked out. Luckily we had a good enough car to finish on the podium." Rookie Tony Kanaan posted a worthy fourth place ahead of Marlboro Penske's Al Unser Jr. in fifth. The race was another virtuoso performance by Zanardi who was unchallenged with a 6.839 second cushion at the finish.

Following the Budweiser/G.I. Joe's 200 Presented by Texaco-Havoline the PPG Cup points leaders were Alex Zanardi, 134, Greg Moore, 96, Jimmy Vasser, 85, Adrian Fernandez, 75, and Gil de Ferran, 55.

First lap fracas takes out Michael Andretti, Christian Fittipaldi, and Greg Moore.

Cheryl Day Anderson

Firestone's Al Speyer stands in front of a sizeable pile of Firehawk Champ Car racing tires,
emblematic of the marque's 18 victories in the 19 race FedEx Championship Series schedule.

Cheryl Day Anderson

FedEx Championship Series Race 10
Medic Drug Grand Prix of Cleveland
Presented by Star Bank
Burke Lakefront Airport
Cleveland, OH
July 12, 1998
100 Laps, 2.106 Mile Road Course

ALEX ZANARDI ZIPS HOME IN THE MEDIC DRUG GRAND PRIX OF CLEVELAND - AGAIN

At the scene of perhaps the finest performance of his three year FedEx Championship career, Alex Zanardi scored a repeat victory on the wide runways of Cleveland's Burke Lakefront Airport circuit, his fifth of the season. While lacking the theatrics of his 1997 "come from behind, way behind" win Zanardi put on his usual good show. He was out-qualified by teammate Jimmy Vasser, who led for the first 11 laps before giving way to Zanardi. The rest of the race belonged to the colorful Italian except for 21 laps in the lead which fell to Christian Fittipaldi. Fittipaldi's out of sequence pit stops cost him any chance of victory and ended him up in 11th place. Michael Andretti, the other half of the Newman-Haas driving pair, while never in the lead, fared better, with a solid second place finish. Unable to put any real pressure on leader Zanardi, Andretti had the difficult assignment of fending off third place Dario Franchitti while trying to conserve fuel. Franchitti tried to get by but didn't have the speed. "There were two places on the track where I could have passed him, but I wasn't quick enough. It was a good result for Team KOOL Green but somebody needs to stop this guy Zanardi. We want to move up to the top step." Scott Pruett and Adrian Fernandez rounded out the top five.

After the Medic Drug Grand Prix of Cleveland Presented by Star Bank the PPG Cup points leaders were Alex Zanardi, 155, Greg Moore, 96, Jimmy Vasser, 92, Adrian Fernandez, 85, and Michael Andretti with 68 points.

Michael C. Brown

FedEx Championship Series Race 11
Molson Indy
Toronto, Ontario, Canada
July 19, 1998
95 Laps, 1.721 Mile Road Course

ALEX ZANARDI MAKES IT FOUR IN A ROW AT TORONTO

No, Alex Zanardi didn't set a record in winning his fourth con- secutive CART race, the 1998 Molson Indy. He did, however, tie the mark set by Al Unser Jr. back in 1990. Al Jr. had a less exciting outing today, qualifying and finishing mid-field. Team KOOL Green's Dario Franchitti appeared to be the class of the field, qualifying on the pole and leading a total of 76 laps of the 95 scheduled, before spinning due to brake problems and ending up 16 laps down. His misfortune handed the lead to Michael Andretti on lap 80. Andretti held out for 13 laps despite having a car that was "loose all day." On lap 92, he gave into unre- lenting pressure from Zanardi, who built up a 1.921 second margin in his last three laps enroute to victory circle. Andretti, no stranger to misfor- tune himself, was sympathetic to Franchitti's bad break. "Poor Dario. He was in a class of his own today. I don't think anybody had anything for him." Jimmy Vasser added to the cheer in the Target-Ganssi camp by capturing the third place on the podi- um, which elevated him to second in the points standings, behind Zanardi who has built up an imposing lead. Teammates Bobby Rahal and Bryan Herta completed the top five.

The PPG Cup points leaders fol- lowing the Molson Indy were Alex Zanardi, 175, Jimmy Vasser, 106, Greg Moore, 98, Adrian Fernandez, 89, and Michael Andretti with 84 points.

FedEx Championship Series Race 12
U.S. 500 Presented by Toyota
Michigan Speedway
Brooklyn, MI
July 26, 1998
250 Laps, 2 Mile Oval

GREG MOORE MAKES LAST LAP PASS ON JIMMY VASSER TO WIN U.S. 500

Greg Moore made a dramatic turnaround in the four race slump that cost him the series' points leadership with a crowd thrilling last lap pass of race leader Jimmy Vasser. He crossed the finish line a mere .259 second ahead of Vasser and a hard charging Alex Zanardi who took down third place. In a race marked by a record 62 lead changes, teammates Vasser and Zanardi had swapped first place ten times in the 21 laps leading up to Moore's eye-opening last lap move. The race's excitement was dulled by an unfortunate accident that cost three spectators' lives when a wheel, off polesitter Adrian Fernandez's crashed car, went into the stands.

After the race Moore recalled his epic move. "Once we got the white flag, I got a good run into turn one. He took the outside, I took the inside. I got a good run down the back straight and was able to hold on. It was an eventful day." Among Moore's events were two stalls in the pits.

The Handford device, a winglike aerodynamic device designed to slow the cars on superspeedways, passed its first test with flying colors, as evidenced by the lower qualifying speeds and the crowd pleasing number of lead changes. Scott Pruett and Richie Hearn were the fourth and fifth place finishers. Moore made his Player's Forsythe team members a happy crew with his spectacular win over the rival Target-Ganassi group.

The U.S. 500 produced the following PPG Cup points leaders: Alex Zanardi, 190, Jimmy Vasser, 122, Greg Moore, 118, Michael Andretti, 92, and Adrian Fernandez, 90.

500 mile classic. At the end, Greg Moore's epic last lap pass made him the winner.

Michael C. Brown

Michael Andretti was only one of Mid-Ohio's multiple crash victims.

FedEx Championship Series Race 13
Miller Lite 200
Mid-Ohio Sports Car Course
Lexington, OH
August 9, 1998
83 Laps, 2.258 Mile Road Course

ADRIAN FERNANDEZ MASTERS MID-OHIO

Adrian Fernandez topped team-mate Scott Pruett and the other 26 starters in the Miller Lite 200 as the point man in a perfect one-two finish for the teammates in the Ford powered Patrick Racing team. While never in the lead, the always aggressive Pruett pushed Fernandez hard over the 26 laps that Fernandez led at the end. Fernandez prevailed by only .247 second at the checker. Greg Moore had a great race going, leading as late as lap 52 until a tangle took him out of contention. Pole-sitter Dario Franchitti and Jimmy Vasser, who started alongside him on the front row, were the principals in a collision that took both of them out without completing a single lap. Third fastest qualifier Bryan Herta also became involved. He kept running for two laps before falling out of the race. Bobby Rahal, saying good-bye as a driver to the track where he got his start, put on a star caliber performance. Though starting 16th, he made his way through the field for a solid third place and a place on the podium, from which he faced a sea of his fans. Rahal said "goodbye" in style, on the track, with 20 laps to go he said to himself, "Let's make them the best 20 laps we've ever had here. I believe we did. I set my fastest lap with three to go. I came away very satisfied with our drive."

After the Miller Lite 200 the PPG Cup points leaders were Alex Zanardi, 190, Jimmy Vasser, 122, Greg Moore, 118, Adrian Fernandez, 110, Michael Andretti, 92, and Scott Pruett, 92.

FedEx Championship Series Race 14
Texaco-Havoline 200
Road America
Elkhart Lake, WI
August 16, 1998
50 Laps, 4.048 Mile Road Course

DARIO FRANCHITTI DOMINATES AT ELKHART LAKE

The Scotsman with the Italian name and driving style to match, carried the Team KOOL Green colors into victory circle for the first time at Elkhart Lake. In a stunning reversal of his first lap crash at Mid-Ohio in his previous outing, he never put a wheel wrong, and at times enjoyed a huge lead of almost half a minute. Not pressed, he enjoyed a 7.102 second cushion over runner-up Alex Zanardi at the finish. Zanardi rebounded strongly from a lap seven tangle with Al Unser Jr. to claim the second spot. Typically, polesitter Michael Andretti had just the opposite kind of luck. While running second on the last lap, Andretti cut a tire and went off course, out of contention. Andretti teammate Christian Fittipaldi, no stranger to bad luck himself, fared better, taking down the third spot in the Kmart Swift Ford. Fourth place went to Rookie Tony Kanaan, while Adrian Fernandez picked up the final spot in the top five. Bryan Herta, the second fastest qualifier, posted a single lap in the lead before being involved in a race ending tangle on lap 11.

Franchitti set the tone for a well earned team celebration. "The guys at Team KOOL Green are going to have a party. The stops were awesome. I hope this is the first of many."

Following the Texaco-Havoline 200 the points leaders were Alex Zanardi, 206, Jimmy Vasser, 126, Adrian Fernandez, 120, Greg Moore, 118, and Michael Andretti with 93 points.

Dario Franchitti dominates at Elkhart Lake,
a first victory for Team KOOL Green.

Michael C. Brown

Big Payoff in Portland... Dario Franchitti wins from the pole, Alex Zanardi Clinches the PPG Cup.

FedEx Championship Series Race 15
Molson Indy Vancouver
Vancouver, British Columbia, Canada
September 6, 1998
86 Laps, 1.802 Mile Road Course

DARIO FRANCHITTI FLASHES TO SECOND CONSECUTIVE WIN AT VANCOUVER

ALEX ZANARDI CLINCHES HIS SECOND CONSECUTIVE CHAMPIONSHIP

Back on the pole and back in the winner's circle, Team KOOL Green's Dario Franchitti proved at Vancouver that he was no one-race wonder, but a serious contender for championship honors in 1999. It's too

late to catch points leader Alex Zanardi this year, he has already nailed down his second PPG Cup in a row, earlier than any CART driver in history. Zanardi started third, finished fourth, gained 12 points, enough for the title. Jimmy Vasser, second in the points parade, took a rare trip into the wall, scored zero for the day. Runner-up Michael Andretti experienced none of the misfortunes that have plagued him this year and throughout his career. He simply wasn't fast enough to match Franchitti, who led the last seven laps as well as the first 21. Scott Pruett took down third place, while fifth went to Al Unser Jr., who moved up smartly from his 22nd starting position. Fast qualifier Bryan Herta again started on the front row, again

saw his chances dissolve in a crash. Rookie Helio Castro-Neves was a mid-race factor, leading 20 laps before encountering fuel problems. Alex Barron put the Toyota powered Gurney Eagle in front for 12 laps before exiting in a tangle.

Franchitti and Zanardi both had big paydays. Franchitti picked up $340,000 in Marlboro Pole Award and bonus money as the first driver to win from the pole in more than a year. Zanardi was assured of the $1 million bonus that goes with the PPG Cup.

The PPG Cup points leaders following the Molson Indy Vancouver were Alex Zanardi, 218, Jimmy Vasser, 126, Adrian Fernandez, 120, Greg Moore, 118, and Dario Franchitti, 110.

FedEx Championship Series Race 16
Honda Grand Prix of Monterey
featuring the Texaco-Havoline 300
Laguna Seca Raceway
Monterey, CA
September 13, 1998
83 Laps, 2.238 Mile Road Course

BRYAN HERTA BESTS ALEX ZANARDI AT MONTEREY

This time Bryan Herta made it stick. In 1996, Alex Zanardi made an off-circuit last lap pass of Herta, who was in the lead, to win at Monterey. In '97, they banged wheels allowing Scott Pruett to sneak by for the victory. This time Herta was again in front and stayed there despite Zanardi's most strenuous efforts to dislodge him. In fact, he was in front for all but two of the race's 83 laps, a virtuoso performance. The victory, Herta's first, had been a long time coming. 71 previous starts, a significant number of them from pole, had produced only a trio of runner-up finishes. Herta's win overshadowed the accomplishment of Rookie Tony Kanaan who made his first podium finish in third place. Dario Franchitti, coming off a two race winning streak, started on the front row, finished fourth, while Jimmy Vasser, Zanardi's teammate, checked in fifth, from third place on the starting grid.

A happy and relieved Herta had this to say post race. "I was fighting, scraping to stay ahead and I don't know how many more laps I would have been able to hold him off. But fate was shining on us today. It means a great deal to me to have raced Alex the way we did today. I regard him as the best driver in the series."

After the Honda Grand Prix of Monterey featuring the Texaco-Havoline 300, the PPG Cup points leaders were Alex Zanardi, 234, Jimmy Vasser, 136, Adrian Fernandez, 126, Dario Franchitti, 122, and Greg Moore, 118.

Michael C. Brown

Dario Franchitti flashes winning form in the rain.

FedEx Championship Series Race 17
Texaco Grand Prix of Houston
Houston, TX
October 4, 1998
70 Laps, 1.527 Mile Road Course

FRANCHITTI WINS RAIN SHORTENED GRAND PRIX OF HOUSTON

It rained on everybody's parade at the Texaco Grand Prix of Houston. Everybody, that is, except for Dario Franchitti. Franchitti started second, quickly moved up front and stayed there during the rain that greeted the start, a short clearing period and the rain, again, with added lightning, that ended the event under caution after 70 laps of the scheduled 100. Not that rain is a problem for Franchitti. He grew up and got his early racing training in Scotland where rain is a way of life. Franchitti's parade was threatened only by teammate Paul Tracy, who bumped Franchitti from the rear on lap 48 while attempting to pass. More often than not it's the bumped car that goes into the wall. This time it was the bumper who spun and tagged the barrier. Franchitti sailed on, unharmed. Needless to say Tracy's reception back in the Team KOOL Green pits was less than cordial. Franchitti went on to build up a lead as large as 11 seconds before the full course yellow flag that led to the checker on lap 70. Already the 1998 champion, Alex Zanardi was the runner-up today, racking up a season total of 250 points, a record with two events yet to come. Rookie Tony Kanaan captured third place, matching his Laguna Seca run and nailed down Rookie of the Year honors plus the accompanying Jim Trueman bonus. Max Papis took down fifth, a best effort for him and Toyota power.

Following the Texaco Grand Prix of Houston the PPG Cup points leaders were Alex Zanardi, 250, Jimmy Vasser, 148, Dario Franchitti, 143, Adrian Fernandez, 134, and Greg Moore, with 119 points.

FedEx Championship Race 18
Honda Indy
Gold Coast, Queensland, Australia
October 18, 1998
62 Laps, 2.795 Mile Road Course

ALEX ZANARDI BACK IN THE WINNER'S CIRCLE AT AUSTRALIA'S HONDA INDY

Rumor has it that two time PPG Cup winner Alex Zanardi is going back to Italy and Formula One in 1999, despite the strenuous efforts of Target-Ganassi's leader Chip Ganassi to retain him. If true, he's going back on a high note, his sev-enth win of the year, a high spirited romp at Surfers Paradise. His total of 15 wins in 50 career starts affords him a winning percentage of .300, the best in CART's history. Dario Franchitti, coming off his Houston win, was on the pole and led the first 13 laps. The rest was all Zanardi, 49 laps in front. Scheduled for 65 laps, the race was shortened to 62 when it ran into CART's two hour limit on road circuits due to a three car crash on lap 60 involving Michael Andretti, Alex Barron, and Helio Castro-Neves. The crash brought out the yellow flag, slowing the pace down, so there wasn't time to finish. Though pressured by runner-up Franchitti at the end, Zanardi appeared to be in no serious danger of losing his lead. Franchitti's 17 points vaulted him into second place in the PPG Cup points over Jimmy Vasser, whose accident today, after 38 laps, left his point total stationary. A workmanlike third place for Christian Fittipaldi erased some bad memories of his 1997 outing here, wherein an accident left him with a broken leg - and an abbreviated season. Zanardi was on target in his post-race comments. "I knew I had the car to do the job. Once I was in front there wasn't much to worry about. I was driving a beautiful race car - which I had all day."

After the Honda Indy, the top contenders in the PPG Cup points race following champion Alex Zanardi with 271 points, were Dario Franchitti, 160, Jimmy Vasser, 148, Adrian Fernandez, 142, and Greg Moore, 124.

Steve Swope

FedEx Championship Series Race 19
Marlboro 500 Presented by Toyota
California Speedway
Fontana, CA
November 1, 1998
250 Laps, 2.029 Mile Oval

A TARGET/GANASSI FIELD DAY AT FONTANA

Target-Ganassi Racing walked away from the high stakes racing game at the Marlboro 500 with all the chips. Jimmy Vasser won the race in a thrilling slingshot pass of Greg Moore on the next to last lap. Vasser picked up a $1 million bonus, and clinched second place in the championship, good for another $500,000 bonus - this one from PPG. Paul Tracy suffered perhaps his worst mis-

fortune in a difficult season. He had been in front for 25 laps when he spun on a restart on lap 246. This put Moore in front (he would have preferred second place) setting the stage for Vasser's winning slingshot pass. Alex Zanardi captured third place, making his season total 285, a mark that may last quite a while. Vasser's leading rival for the year's runner-up honors, Dario Franchitti, suffered a rare engine failure and was demoted to third place in the year's totals. He remains along with Vasser, and Moore, the year's fifth place points producer, a leading contender for top honors in 1999, now that Zanardi has officially confirmed his departure. Adrian Fernandez took fourth place in the race and in the championship. Mauricio Gugelmin was the final driver in the day's top five.

Bobby Rahal, in his farewell appearance as a Champ Car driver, finished 11th, good for tenth place in the season's standings. It was the 16th time Rahal, a three time champion, had finished in the year's top ten. Becoming a full time car owner in '99, Rahal had a wry comment on his new driver team, incumbent Bryan Herta and Rahal replacement Max Papis. They had a run-in on lap 39 that took them both out of the race. "I had already introduced Max to Bryan sometime ago. I didn't think he'd feel the need to do it again."

The top ten in the final season standings following the Marlboro 500 were Alex Zanardi, 285, Jimmy Vasser, 169, Dario Franchitti, 160, Adrian Fernandez, 154, Greg Moore, 140, Scott Pruett, 161, Michael Andretti, 112, Bryan Herta, 97, Tony Kanaan, 92, and Bobby Rahal, 92.

Cheryl Day Anderson

Now It's Businessman Bobby... Not that Bobby Rahal wasn't all business in the cockpit. You don't win three PPG Cups, two of them back-to-back, 24 Champ Car races, the Indianapolis 500, the Daytona 24 Hours, and the Sebring 12 Hours without being focused. The driving part of his multifaceted career came to a close at Fontana's season ending event with a trackside salute from the assembled members of all the teams on the FedEx Championship Series circuit. Now he can concentrate on his Champ Car racing team with drivers Bryan Herta and new hire Max Papis, his NASCAR Craftsman Truck racing team (with partner Tom Gloy), his automotive dealerships, and his corporate directorships which include CART. If that sounds like a lot, be assured that Rahal can handle it.

Get Ready To Kick Some Asphalt!

UNI-T® Technology. Driving Dayton® To A New Standard Of Performance.

At Dayton, we challenge our tires to meet the punishing demands of Indy Lights championship racing and push them to provide performance for every road. The same spirit that has made us a winner on the track is driving us to deliver the winning edge in passenger tire performance. The result of this relentless dedication to performance can be seen in two new Dayton high performance tires: the Daytona® ZR and the Daytona® HR, both featuring **UNI-T**—the **U**ltimate **N**etwork of **I**ntelligent **T**ire Technology! Call 1-888-597-8597 or visit our web site at www.daytontire.com for your nearest retailer.

Daytona ZR With UNI-T

▶ Z-Speed rated.

▶ Three noticeably wide grooves help resist hydroplaning.

▶ Directional slots and sipes help evacuate water to enhance performance.

▶ Advanced noise-canceling technology.

▶ Rim Guard™ on 17″ sizes.

Daytona HR With UNI-T

▶ H-Speed rated.

▶ Three noticeably wide grooves help resist hydroplaning.

▶ Directional slots and sipes help evacuate water to enhance performance.

▶ Advanced noise-canceling technology.

What Is UNI-T Technology?
UNI-T, the **U**ltimate **N**etwork of **I**ntelligent **T**ire Technology, is a total rethinking of the automobile tire combining three principle technologies.

CO-CS® Innovative Tire Design
 • A Comprehensive Tire Design Method

O-Bead® Innovative Roundness
 • Rounder Is Better

L.L. Carbon® Innovative New Compound
 • Longer Is Stronger

Ultimate Tire Technology

Daytona® ZR With UNI-T®   Daytona® HR With UNI-T®

FINISH LINE PERFORMANCE

www.daytontire.com
Retailer Locator # 1-888-597-8597

PPG-DAYTON INDY LIGHTS
A Banner Year... Cristiano da Matta Takes the Title and Lands Champ Car Ride for '99. Transition to CART Ownership and Dayton Tires Goes Smoothly.

A prime purpose of Indy Lights is to graduate drivers (and teams) to the major leagues; CART's Champ Car circuit. Two '97 Lights drivers who made the jump, Tony Kanaan and Alex Barron distinguished themselves in their freshman year on the senior circuit. 1997 champion Kanaan even made the top ten in CART's FedEx Championship. Top of the class of '98 was Brazilian Cristiano da Matta who landed with Arciero-Wells for 1999. Da Matta was the fourth driver in five years of Lights competition to win the championship for Steve Horne's Tasman Motorsports. He chalked up four victories, three poles, and 154 points, clinched the title at Vancouver with two races to go. Guy Smith, a Britisher, and Japan's Shigeaki Hattori each posted a pair of wins. The other winners were Didier Andre of France, Brazilians Airton Dare and Luiz Garcia Jr., Irishman Derek Higgins, and Americans Tony Renna and Mark Hotchkis. If the lineup of race winners sounds like the UN, the total driver lineup was even more international with Mexicans and Australians added. This international flavor is testimony to Indy Lights' appeal to young drivers from all over the world as the best stepping stone to Champ Cars. Once there, it can be on to Formula One, as two recent Champ Car titleists have done.

Rookie of the Year in '97, da Matta, like the series itself, had a banner year. In addition to his four victories, he scored three poles and four fastest race laps. Da Matta started the season on a tear; runner-up at Homestead, back-to-back wins at Long Beach and Nazareth, and a third at Gateway. After a desultory tenth at Milwaukee he bounded back up to second at Detroit. His next three races were marked by a pair of crashes and an engine failure. On the rebound, the Brazilian was the runner-up at Michigan, and ran away with two Canadian events, Trois Rivieres and Vancouver, from the pole. After clinching the title at Vancouver, his last two outings of the year were relatively low key and, indeed, added little to his points total.

Runner-up for the title, Didier Andre scored 125 points on consistency - and a big win at Laguna Seca. He was a huge .773 second faster than any other driver in qualifying there and, indeed, led from pole-to-pole, with little significant opposition. Andre is expected back in '99 and, based on his performance at Laguna Seca alone, he should be a contender for the championship.

Rookie of the Year - and indeed a serious title contender for a while - was British Formula 3 graduate Guy Smith. He ended up third in the points parade with 110, after coming within ten points of leader da Matta at one stage. Having never seen an oval from the cockpit before the season opening at Homestead event, Smith provided evidence of his learning ability and speed - with a third place finish. Over the next five races the learning curve got steeper and eighth (twice) was the best he could do. At Portland, however, the British youngster found a course to his liking and claimed the pole. He went on to win despite an off course excursion just after the start. Then came a fourth at Cleveland and another winning flag-to-flag romp at Toronto. That was the highpoint of his season.

The third Giaffone to race in the Lights series, Felipe, took down fourth place in the series with 104 points. The Brazilian failed to win, but three second places show that he has the potential to claim the top place on the podium. Like Andre and Smith he's expected back, with the same team, which should be helpful.

An Irish driver with a Mexican team, Quaker State/Team GO, Derek Higgins mastered the Milwaukee Mile in a winning outing and notched a pair of runner-up slots for fifth place in the year's campaign at 94 points. He'd like to return in '99 but, at season's end, had no assured ride.

Airton Dare, da Matta's teammate at Tasman, was outshone by the champion-to-be most of the year. Dare qualified on the pole at Detroit, jumped out in front at the start and was never headed. Over the rest of the year, a third place at Vancouver was his best finish. His 78 points landed him in sixth place on the leader board at season's end. He, too, is a likely returnee for '99.

Spain's Oriol Servia picked up a pair of second places late in the season. They were the highlights of his 73 point year, good for seventh place in the series.

American Tony Renna had proven his speed in previous Lights campaigns and was expected to be a major factor in this one. Unhappily, he crashed heavily in practice at Homestead and got off to a bad start. He didn't really get going until Michigan where he was on the pole and prevailed at the end. He missed Vancouver but was again on the pole at Fontana and scored a solid third place there. His fast but uneven season produced 68 points, good for eighth place in the standings.

Another American, Geoff Boss, showed less speed but a lot more consistency, including a third place and a second place which added up to 67 points and ninth place.

The Hattori claiming the last place in the top ten wasn't double race winner Shigeaki (He turned up further down in 14th place.) but Naoki, no relative, whose best three races consisted of a pair of third places and one runner-up slot. Naoki's consistency added up to 66 points.

With nine different winners, a record, and 15 race leaders, perhaps the only thing lacking in a stellar season was more passing action at the front. Half the races were won by a polesitter who was never passed. The transition of ownership of the series to Championship Auto Racing Teams and the switch to Bridgestone/Firestone's Dayton brand as the spec tire went smoothly.

Cristiano da Matta - Clear cut champion, scored four wins, three poles, wrapped up the title early, with two races to go. He's headed for the Arciero-Wells Champ Car team in '99. (150 PPG-Dayton Indy Lights points)

2 **Andre Didier** - Points producing consistency plus one spectacular win at Laguna Seca gained him the runner-up slot. (125 PPG-Dayton Indy Lights points)

3 **Guy Smith** - Grabbed Rookie of the Year honors, at midyear was only ten points behind the overall leader. Two victories as a freshman indicate championship potential for '99. (110 PPG-Dayton Indy Light points)

Cheryl Day Anderson

4 **Felipe Giaffone** - The third member of his family in the series, didn't quite make victory lane, but scored three runner-up finishes. (104 PPG-Dayton Indy Lights points)

5 **Derek Higgins** - An Irish driver on a Mexican team mastered the Milwaukee Mile, added two runner-up finishes but may be looking for a '99 ride. (94 PPG-Dayton Indy Lights points)

Dayton's Joe Barbieri can afford to smile at the first year performance of the brand as the spec tire on the PPG-Dayton Indy Lights circuit. The switch went seamlessly.

PPG-Dayton Indy Lights Race 1
Homestead Motorsports Complex
Homestead, FL
March 15, 1998
67 Laps, 100 Miles

SHIGEAKI HATTORI SURPRISES WITH HOMESTEAD WIN

Never a winner in his two previous Indy Lights seasons, or even a podium occupant, Japan's Shigeaki Hattori turned heads with his commanding victory in the Homestead opener. He was second on the starting grid to Brazil's Sergio Paese, whose pole was also somewhat of a surprise. Hattori went around Paese on lap four. Paese, who had found the wall in practice, found it again while attempting to repass Hattori on lap 29. Paese blamed Hattori for pinching him down below the white line and his subsequent spin. "Not a good guy," was the label he applied to Hattori. Hattori denied any improper moves. When green resumed, first Rahal protégé Mike Borkowski, then Felipe Giaffone, Naoki Hattori, Airton Dare, and Jorge Goeters hit different sections of the turn four wall. Through it all, Hattori motored on to the checker unperturbed, his only pressure, and that of a very mild variety, coming from Cristiano da Matta, the runner-up. Britisher Guy Smith proved a quick study of oval tracks, finishing third the first time he ever raced on one. Oriol Servia of Spain and Chris Simmons, the first American finishers, were fourth and fifth.

PPG-Dayton Indy Lights Race 2
Long Beach Street Circuit
Long Beach, CA
April 5, 1998
47 Laps, 74 Miles

CRISTIANO DA MATTA CRUISES TO LONG BEACH VICTORY

Cristiano da Matta took a conservative approach to the season opener at Homestead, opting for a secure second place rather than driving for the win. Not this time out. Da Matta blasted by polesitter Didier Andre at the start and led every lap on the way to his first victory of the year. He was .459 second ahead of runner-up Geoff Boss. The margin would have been larger but for the lap 42 spin of Rodolfo Lavin which brought out the yellow flag. Da Matta had built up as much as a three second lead at one point. Boss, along with Naoki Hattori and Philipp Peter, had passed Andre when his car was slowing. ("Jumping out of gear," he said.) Andre eventually grazed the wall and salvaged a fifth place finish. Da Matta, the winner of three events in '97, noted post race that it was a relief to get his first win for his new team Tasman Motorsports. "Always when you join a new team, you want to prove yourself." Based on today's convincing performance, his first win of 1998 will be only one of many.

PPG-Dayton Indy Lights Race 3
Nazareth Speedway
Nazareth, PA
April 25, 1998
100 Laps, 95 Miles

CRISTIANO DA MATTA IN CONTROL AT NAZARETH

Cristiano da Matta cruised to the Long Beach win in his previous outing; he cruised even more luxuriously at the usually hotly contested Nazareth race, more than 14 seconds ahead at the checker. On the pole, he jumped off to a clean start in front of the lead pack, progressively building up his cushion. Oriol Servia was next in line, followed by Clint Mears and Philipp Peter, who were vigorously contesting third place. A failed attempt by Peter to get around Mears ended with the Aussie driver in the wall and Mears spinning unharmed. During the long caution brought out by this incident, the officials ruled that Servia had passed a backmarker. The penalty involved called for Servia to drive through the pits. He ended up doing it twice, since the first time under yellow didn't count. A result of this action was the effective removal of da Matta's closest pursuers. Didier Andre came on strong to take second place at the end and, along with it, second place in the championship with 27 points. Da Matta continues to lead the title chase with 59.

The Mears family recouped somewhat with cousin Casey's surge to finish third, ahead of Brian Cunningham and Airton Dare.

Michael C. Brown

PPG-Dayton Indy Lights Race 4
Gateway International Raceway
Madison, IL
May 22, 1998
79 Laps, 100 Miles

SHIGEAKI HATTORI GRABS GATEWAY WIN

No one race wonder, 34 year old Shigeaki Hattori, the series' oldest pilot, proved to be the fastest at Gateway's oval. Late in the race he was ahead by a full six seconds, but two cautions cut his winning margin down to .626 second, a decisive cushion in itself. Hattori started on the front row alongside fastest qualifier Jorge Goeters. The early lead went to Australian Philipp Peter, who was stalked by Hattori and eventually gave up the point to the smooth, swift Japanese driver. Peter did manage to hold on to second place ahead of points leader Cristiano da Matta, whose third place today consolidated his total at 73, a considerable cushion over Hattori's next best 44. Da Matta has made the podium in every outing this year. Felipe Giaffone garnered fourth place and Jorge Goeters, whose pole was somewhat of a surprise, salvaged fifth. Hattori is bidding for a Champ Car ride in 1999.

PPG-Dayton Indy Lights Race 5
The Milwaukee Mile
West Allis, WI
May 30, 1998
97 Laps, 100 Miles

DEREK HIGGINS HANDLES THE FIELD AT MILWAUKEE

Irishman Derek Higgins, a Lights Rookie with no oval track experience prior to this year, surprised the Lights brigade, and possibly himself, by winning on the venerable Milwaukee Mile. It was only his fourth oval outing and he made it look like he grew up on them. Starting seventh, Higgins sliced through the leaders to take command at the halfway mark. In the second half the Team GO driver piled up a husky winning margin of 6.241 seconds over Felipe Giaffone of Brazil. Another Brazilian, polesitter Sergio Paese, held on for third place at the checker. Americans have been shut out of the winner's circle so far this season, but two of them, Geoff Boss and Tony Renna, checked in with the fourth and fifth places. The other Team GO driver, Mexican Jorge Goeters, finished sixth today after taking the pole at Gateway. Higgins met the Team GO group in their Mexican homeland while taking that country's Formula 3 championship twice.

PPG-Dayton Indy Lights Race 6
Raceway on Belle Isle Park
Detroit, MI
June 7, 1998
32 Laps, 75 Miles

TASMAN TWO STEP: AIRTON DARE EDGES CRISTIANO DA MATTA IN DETROIT

In the top drawer Tasman team's 1998 driver lineup, Airton Dare had been taking an early season back seat to Cristiano da Matta, winner of two races and the clear points leader. Not in Detroit. Dare qualified on the pole and got off cleanly for the lead. Nobody else got close, not even da Matta, the second fastest qualifier, who let himself get boxed in at the start and shuffled back to fifth. By the closing stages da Matta was back up to second and cut Dare's mid-race lead of five seconds down to .856 second. At no point did da Matta challenge Dare on the difficult to pass Belle Isle Park circuit. "Don't take each other out," was the entirely reasonable team order of the day. In the year's best showing for American drivers Geoff Boss and Mark Hotchkis placed third and fourth. Didier Andre was the fifth man in the top five. Of note in Tasman Motorsports' big day is that it was a repeat of the 1997 Detroit outing in which Tony Kanaan and Helio Castro-Neves finished one-two. Tasman appears poised for another year on top of Indy Lights.

PPG-Dayton Indy Lights Race 7
Portland International Raceway
Portland, OR
June 21, 1998
38 Laps. 75 Miles

GUY SMITH AND CONTROVERSY RULE AT PORTLAND

Complaints, quite a few but certainly not all directed at winner Guy Smith, abounded at Portland. The brouhaha started right after the green flag waved for the second time; the first start was waved off as uneven. Polesitter Smith, in the lead, went too deep into the first corner, shot off course, short circuited the chicane, got back on the track. Didier Andre followed Smith off course. Geoff Boss bunted points leader Cristiano da Matta into a spin which tagged Oriol Servia. The other Boss, Andy, belted Philipp Peter's car, which caught on fire. Mike Borkowski and Naoki Hattori also managed to get into the act and went off course. Lap 30 saw a lesser confrontation. Backmarker Rodolfo Lavin appeared to be holding up a line of cars attempting to pass him. Tony Renna went off course in his attempt. Andy Boss and Naoki Hattori then collected each other for a field-bunching yellow. Later Lavin spun on his own, bringing out a race ending yellow, with Smith still in command, now only by .497 second. Tasman Motorsports protested that Smith had benefitted from his short circuit of the chicane, a view held by others. The officials ruled otherwise and the results; Smith first, Felipe Giaffone second, Luiz Garcia Jr. third, Airton Dare fourth, and Brian Cunningham fifth were allowed to stand.

Cheryl Day Anderson

PPG-Dayton Indy Lights Race 8
Burke Lakefront Airport
Cleveland, OH
July 12, 1998
36 Laps, 75 Miles

LUIZ GARCIA JR. GRABS THE WIN IN CLEVELAND

Cleveland's wide front straight and turn one afforded the Lights brigade the room they need to get through the first corner without incident, unlike the multicar mixup at Portland, the previous circuit. Polesitter Luiz Garcia Jr. led the way on the first lap and all of the 35 that followed. Oriol Servia was the second fastest qualifier, ahead of points leader Cristiano da Matta. Servia salvaged sixth at the end but da Matta had a bad luck outing, engine failure consigning him to dead last, with only 12 laps completed. His points cushion remained essentially intact with 92 markers compared to new runner-up Guy Smith at 60. Smith was fourth today. Garcia teammate Sergio Paese had a busy day at the office. Paese fumbled his attempt to pass his teammate on lap two and dropped three places. On lap 20, another failed Paese passing attempt, on Oriol Servia, caused both to spin. On reentering the track Paese nailed Geoff Boss in the side. For his heroics, he ended up down a lap. Derek Higgins, the runner-up, made no meaningful move on Garcia and third place Didier Andre didn't threaten Higgins. American Tony Renna finished fifth.

PPG-Dayton Indy Lights Race 9
Toronto Street Circuit
Toronto, Ontario, Canada
July 19, 1998
43 Laps, 75 Miles

GUY SMITH GOES WIRE-TO-WIRE

England's Guy Smith has a simple race strategy: qualify on the pole, jump out in front at the start, stay there til the checker waves. Just as he had at Portland, Smith carried out his plan to a winning conclusion at Toronto. This time there were no multiple off course excursions, no multiple car crashes, no long yellows as had been the case in Portland. In fact, there were no yellows at all, and no protests. Naoki Hattori provided Smith's stiffest opposition. He tried a risky outside pass on lap nine, failed to make it, but caused no damage to himself or Smith and eventually set-

tled for second place. On the first lap, points leader Cristiano da Matta crunched Didier Andre from the rear, lost his front wing and was shuffled to the back of the pack, where he finished, the last driver on the lead lap. This miscue cost him heavily in the campaign for the championship. Winner Smith is now only ten points in arrears and appears to be on a roll. Chris Simmons finished a solid third, followed by Philipp Peter and Didier Andre.

PPG-Dayton Indy Lights Race 10
Michigan Speedway
Brooklyn, MI
July 25, 1998
50 Laps, 100 Miles

TONY RENNA MASTERS MICHIGAN'S HIGH BANKS

What a great place for a Rookie's first win; the daunting high banks of Michigan. First year campaigner Tony Renna qualified at a lofty 184.054 mph and survived the drafting wars that escalated speeds over the 190 mph mark. Sergio Paese set the fastest race lap at 191.954 mph on his way to a third place finish. Cristiano da Matta pulled out of his two race slump with a fine second place which increased his point lead over Guy Smith (108 to 90). Smith finished sixth today. Fans expecting a last lap shoot out

between the leaders in the front draft were disappointed when Mike Borkowski and Airton Dare collided on lap 48 and the race ended under yellow. Clint Mears, of the Mears clan, ran as high as second before he tagged Jorge Goeters in the rear end and faded to eighth. Fourth place went to Andy Boss, which coupled with Renna's win, made it the best day of the year for American drivers. Oriol Servia was the fifth man in the top five.

PPG-Dayton Indy Lights Race 11
Trois-Rivieres Street Circuit
Trois-Rivieres, Canada
August 2, 1998
50 Laps, 75 Miles

CRISTIANO DA MATTA ROMPS TO TROIS-RIVIERES TRIUMPH

Although he denied it afterward, Cristiano da Matta's return to form and victory circle at Trois-Rivieres looked easy. He started on the pole, was never really pressed, finished eased up with a 1.31 second advantage over Oriol Servia. The start was ragged, the first attempt being waved off. The second attempt at green was held up when Airton Dare came to a halt in the middle of the track with a failed transmission. Tony Renna and Derek Higgins, mistakenly thinking the green had waved, collided. By lap five the race was truly underway but shortly thereafter Renna went straight into a barrier with broken steering. Higgins was blamed for the incident by the officials who hit him with a 30 second post-race penalty. Shigeaki Hattori, Mike Borkowski, and Sergio Paese all were involved in accidents which put them out for the day. After the fourth and final caution of the race, there were eight incident-free green flag laps left, which saw Naoki Hattori, Guy Smith, and Didier Andre finish in that order to round out the top five. With only three races left, da Matta's lead over Smith (130-102) is beginning to look more comfortable.

Cheryl Day Anderson

PPG-Dayton Indy LIghts Race 12
Vancouver Street Circuit
Vancouver, Canada
September 6, 1998
47 Laps, 75 Miles

CRISTIANO DA MATTA CRUISES TO VANCOUVER VICTORY, CLINCHES CHAMPIONSHIP

Even Cristiano da Matta himself admitted that, "This race was not so difficult." As he had twice previously, the Brazilian was on the pole and away to a huge lead, this time, as large as six seconds enroute to the checker unchallenged. His winning margin was 3.546 seconds despite a late race yellow that left only two green flag laps before the checker. Runner-up Derek Higgins conceded that he was no threat to the winner. Da Matta's post-race 152 points versus Guy Smith's next best 107 means that the Brazilian's championship is secure despite the outcome of the remaining two outings. Higgins was happy with second place; he's ride hunting for '99 despite a fine freshman year in the series. Da Matta's teammate Airton Dare copped third place, making a handsome showing for Tasman Motorsports. Mike Borkowski, the Bobby Rahal protégé from whom more had been expected preseason, made his best showing of the year in fourth place, with fifth going to Felipe Giaffone.

PPG-Dayton Indy Lights Race 13
Laguna Seca Raceway
Monterey, CA
September 13, 1998
34 Laps, 75 Miles

DIDIER ANDRE SCORES IN DOMINANT DRIVE AT LAGUNA SECA

Didier Andre had the scorers and his competition checking their watches when he posted a .776 second faster qualifying time than any driver at Laguna Seca. They didn't need watches to see that he was way ahead of the field (up to seven seconds) at mid-race. Despite a late race caution he still finished 2.719 seconds ahead of runner-up Oriol Servia, unpressed. Derek Higgins had a busy day enroute to third place. On lap 13 he tried to pass new champion Cristiano da Matta on the inside. Instead, he hit the curb and bounced into da Matta's car. Da Matta got bounced down about five places in the order. He later banged wheels with Luiz Garcia Jr. and went out with steering bothers. Higgins soldiered on to third place. Guy Smith finished fourth but failure to honor a black flag on the next to last lap cost him a 20 second penalty from the officials, good only for a 15th place official finish. This move allowed Geoff Boss and Naoki Hattori to claim the fourth and fifth finishing slots. Happily for da Matta, he already had his championship won.

PPG-Dayton Indy Lights Race 14
California Speedway
Fontana, CA
October 31, 1998
50 Laps, 100 Miles

MARK HOTCHKIS MAKES HIS FINAL LIGHTS RIDE A WINNING ONE AT CALIFORNIA

Prior to the race Mark Hotchkis, who had 43 previous Indy Lights starts, only five of them in 1998, announced he wasn't coming back in '99. Champ Cars maybe, NASCAR Trucks possibly, but not Indy LIghts. In the race, he announced that he's a solid candidate for employment in whatever series he targets, by winning at California in convincing style. The race was all Hotchkis and teammate Tony Renna, the polesitter, who traded the lead six times. Only Cory Witherill, with a pair of singleton leading laps, broke up the intra-team duel. With three laps to go, Hotchkis passed Renna for the last time enroute to victory. Felipe Giaffone snuck by Renna, too, to take runner-up honors leaving Renna to salvage third place. Cory Witherill had fourth place to show for his strong effort. Didier Andre captured fifth place, good enough to elevate him to runner-up status in the championship over Guy Smith who barely made the day's top ten. The day was marked by flat out, draft dominated racing as witness 15th placed Airton Dare in the second pack who posted a 192.5 mph lap, the race's fastest and Indy Lights' fastest ever.

NASCAR WINSTON CUP

DRIVERS

By Benny Phillips

The old woman in black stirred the boiling liquid with a wooden spoon and laughed, a cackling laughter that shook the moss and vibrated the marsh of the Louisiana bayou.

She tossed all the decals and Mark Martin memorabilia into the stew. A swirl of smoke rose from the pot and dissipated among the tree branches overhead. In the distance, a wildcat screamed, and nearby a huge owl answered the challenge.

Nobody seemed to notice, not even the dozen or so Martin fans who, after everything else failed, had turned to voodoo for an answer as to when Jeff Gordon's winning streak would end, allowing Martin, their hero, a Winston Cup championship.

The old witch of the swamp tasted her stew and laughed again. "He is beyond all magic," she said. "There is nothing I can do. Mr. Gordon has all the lucky charms, including the one rabbit's foot that counts most. I tell you, fate must run its course. The end of the lucky streak will eventually come, as it always does, but your driver, Mr. Martin, and all the others, will have to wait."

Mark Martin himself wonders if his day will ever come. Martin managed to drive Jack Roush's Ford Taurus to a handsome seven victories in the debut season for the new Ford Taurus, but still finished a whopping 364 points behind Gordon in the series point race.

Picking up 13 of the 16 victories

scored by the Chevrolet nameplate, Gordon's DuPont team carried the banner for the bowtie throughout the season. The 27 year old driver ran his career record to 42 Winston Cup victories and three championships in only six years on the circuit. Gordon posted an amazing 26 top-five finishes during the 33 race season and finished in the top ten in 28 races. He failed to finish only two events and completed 98.9 percent of all laps run.

Martin, meanwhile, scored 22 top-five finishes and 26 top tens, while only failing to finish one race. His average finish was 8.64, while Gordon's was an incredible 5.70.

"It was a good season for us," Martin said when it was over. I don't know what we could have done different. I face limitations every day, and I don't know how I'm capable of doing more. We took some hits, sure - 30th at Darlington and 40th or so at Talladega in both races. At Talladega, I was involved in wrecks in both races. I had nothing to do with them. I was just a victim who was caught up in the mess. By the same token, I won at Las Vegas, and I should not even have finished the race. My transmission gave up with a few laps to go, and had there been a few more laps, I would not have made it."

But his fans, and they are many, still seek an answer, even from voodoo queens.

"I'm satisfied I did the best I could do in 1998," Martin said. "I suppose it is a matter of what you

do within a certain time frame. When Dale Earnhardt was the man and was winning all the races and the championships, I ran second to him in points, and now Gordon is the man and I'm second to him. I don't know if I will ever be *the* man, but I hope I will. Maybe in 1999."

The voodoo lady said fate must run its course. While Richard Petty, king of NASCAR racing, doesn't believe in any primitive religion based on sorcery, he does subscribe to the theory that Gordon will be hot until his time runs out.

"Jeff Gordon was the driver to beat in 1998, and chances are good he will be the driver to beat in '99," Petty said.

"These things are difficult to explain, but when you're hot you're hot, and when you're not you're not."

"Bill Elliott was that way in 1985, '87, and '88. Everybody figured that nobody could beat him. He won 11 races in '85, six in '87, and six more in '88. Earnhardt had good streaks, too, or he would not have won seven championships. He won 11 races in '87, and nine in '90 and six in '93. I had some good streaks, too, during my driving career. I won 27 races in 1967, including ten straight," Petty said.

"Darrell Waltrip won 12 races in 1981 and a dozen more in '82. Rusty Wallace has had some good runs, and so has Mark Martin. The point is, not a single one of us can give you a really good answer as to why. Gordon can't, either. Gordon is smart enough to know that he better get it all while he can, because when that little hole opens in the sack, everything pours out a lot faster than it went in the sack. Nothing goes on forever, and what goes up must come down," Petty contends.

Meanwhile, Gordon is basking in the sun. He won his second consecutive series title and third in four years. Teammate Terry Labonte won the championship in 1996. Put it together and Hendrick Motorsports has reached dynasty status with four straight championships.

Gordon tied Petty's modern-era, single-season victory mark in winning the 13 races. Also, Gordon twice picked up $1 million bonuses from R.J. Reynolds via its No Bull 5 bonus program and set a single-season earnings mark of $6,175,867, excluding the championship award of more than $2 million.

"The type of year I had is unbelievable," Gordon admitted. "To me just winning races is all it takes, then when I look at the races that we won and the way that we won them and then to wrap it up with a championship is incredible. What we have accomplished over the last three of four years is incredible."

Gordon praised his crew, led by pit boss Ray Evernham. He credited the team with everything. "I think the thing that goes overlooked is the combination of me and Ray and this entire team," Gordon said. "We have people who have been here for a long time. They all work like a fine tuned machine or a fine watch. All the pieces go together, and everything goes like clockwork. When you have that, it is hard to beat. Sometimes you can overcome a lot of things when people are working together."

Gordon talked about Martin. "I think Mark Martin is one of the hardest driving individuals I've ever raced against, and one of the most intense drivers on and off the track. That's why I have so much respect for him and feel our accomplishments in 1998 are better than ever, because of having to race against Mark for the championship. Yet, having a year like 1998 gets me going. It was one of the most fun years I've ever had dri-

ving a race car, and it just blows me away that it happened on a level such as Winston Cup."

The track didn't seem to matter. Gordon did well everywhere, winning the first restrictor-plate race under the lights at Daytona in October and sweeping the road course events at Sears Point and Watkins Glen. He also won on half mile, mile, 1.5 mile, 2 mile, and 2.5 mile ovals.

Gordon won his first race of the year in the second race of the season at Rockingham. Then he won at Bristol, followed by Charlotte in the 600. His big run during the year came during July and August when he won four straight races, including his second victory in the Brickyard 400 at Indianapolis Motor Speedway, earning him the first of his two $1 million bonuses with a triumph in the Southern 500 at Darlington.

Gordon's wins, in the order they were posted included: Rockingham, Bristol, Charlotte, Sears Point, Pocono, Indianapolis, Watkins Glen, Michigan, New Hampshire, Darlington, Daytona, Rockingham, and Atlanta.

Martin gave chase all season, and Dale Jarrett, who drove Robert Yates' Ford, chased Martin and Gordon. Jarrett, who won three races during the year, finished third in the point standings. He won a $1 million No Bull bonus victory at Talladega, and posted 19 top fives and 22 top tens. He completed the final two races despite spending several days in the hospital after the Phoenix race because of gallstones. He had successful surgery after the season.

Rusty Wallace was a contender most of the season, but did not win a race until Phoenix late in the season. Wallace posted 15 top fives and 21 top tens. Wallace and new teammate Jeremy Mayfield benefited from the new two-car Penske South arrangement. Mayfield posted the first top ten points finish of his career, ending up seventh. He also won his first Winston Cup race at Pocono and collected a dozen top fives and 16 top tens. Both Penske drivers were in Fords.

Jeff Burton, Martin's teammate with Roush, finished fifth in points, picking up two victories along the

way. Burton beat Gordon at Richmond in a side-by-side finish.

Bobby Labonte carried the Pontiac banner, posting two victories enroute to a sixth place finish in points. Labonte's effort was the best by a single car team.

And, after 19 years of trying, Dale Earnhardt finally won the Daytona 500. His dramatic victory set the tone for NASCAR's 50th anniversary celebration. It was to be his only triumph of the season. He finished eighth in points and posted just five top five finishes and 13 runs inside the top ten.

Terry Labonte, the 1984 and 1996 champion, was as consistent as ever and finished ninth in points. He drove the Hendrick Motorsports Chevrolet to one victory, five top fives and 15 top tens.

Bobby Hamilton, in his first year with Morgan-McClure Motorsports, finished the year strong and beat John Andretti and Ken Schrader for tenth place in the standings. Hamilton dominated at Martinsville in the spring race and added three top fives and eight top ten efforts.

Ricky Rudd was the only other driver to win a race. He finished first at Martinsville in September. The victory extended his winning streak to 16 straight seasons.

NASCAR also made its first venture to Las Vegas Motor Speedway in March, and the Winston Cup series will make an inaugural visit to Homestead Motorsports Park in 1999, bringing the schedule to 34 events.

The one thing that was missing in Gordon's climb in 1998 was the team's most important player, Rick Hendrick, who was at home struggling with leukemia, and under court order resulting from legal charges stemming from his automobile dealerships and sales business. Hendrick wasn't allowed any role in his team in '98. His brother John took over the racing operation for the year. Now Rick will be back in 1999, which should add even more strength to Gordon's chances.

He's on a roll and who's to stop him? The voodoo lady down in the bayou says it will take time. That's probably as good an answer as you're going to get.

Nigel Kinrade

Jeff Gordon - "An unbelievable year," admits Gordon himself after winning his second Winston Cup in a row. 13 wins, 26 top fives, two $1 million Winston No Bull bonuses included in record single season earnings of $6,175,867 (exclusive of the $2 million+ championship award). Unbelievable, unless you're Jeff Gordon.

2 **Mark Martin** - Seven victories and 22 top five finishes, good enough for the title most years, but not in 1998. Martin needs move up only one notch to take his first Winston Cup in 1999 but will the 1997 and '98 titleist move over?

3 **Dale Jarrett** - A determined title pursuit netted three victories and 19 top fives, good for third place in the year's standings. A $1 million Winston No Bull bonus at Talladega alleviated some of the disappointment. Though in pain, a gallant Jarrett postponed gall bladder surgery til after the season ended.

4 Rusty Wallace - A contender most of the season, but not a winner until Phoenix late in the year. 15 top fives helped salvage fourth place at season end. His four poles, including a record run at Dover, made him one of the year's top qualifiers.

5 **Jeff Burton** - Martin's teammate at Roush Racing picked up two wins, including edging Gordon at Richmond, has title potential for 1999. Burton has finished in the year's top five for the past three seasons, reinforcing his stature.

Nigel Kinrade

6 **Bobby Labonte** - The prime Pontiac pilot won three of the four poles at Daytona and Talladega, and one of the races, Daytona's Pepsi 400. Consistency was lacking however, as marked by nine finishes of 20th or worse. Car owner Joe Gibbs planned concerted efforts on this item in the off-season.

Nigel Kinrade

7 **Jeremy Mayfield** - Only one win, in the Pocono 500, but Mayfield actually led the Winston Cup points parade at one point. With Rusty Wallace as teammate, the Penske South duo makes a powerful pair. He also scored one pole, at Texas, but was bogged down by a rash of subpar finishes.

8 **Dale Earnhardt** - Earnhardt at long last chased down the one trophy missing from his mantelpiece, the Daytona 500. His loyal fans hoped that a record eighth Winston Cup would follow. It was not to be, with a third at Phoenix his second best 1998 finish.

Nigel Kinrade

9 **Terry Labonte** - Consistency was Labonte's middle name in his 1996 Championship year. Not in 1998, when he had a half dozen finishes near the bottom of the pack. He did win at Richmond and kept his top ten standing for the 16th year.

10 **Bobby Hamilton** - An undersung campaigner, Hamilton scored a victory, Martinsville, for the third year in a row, made the year's top ten for the second time in the last three years. His 1998 victory was from the pole, his first.

John Andretti - No wins this year, but three top five finishes and ten top tens for Richard Petty's driver added up to much improved consistency and a year end standing just outside the top ten points producers.

12 **Ken Schrader** - Always a top qualifier, Schrader again notched two poles in 1998. With three top five finishes and 11 top tens, he just made Winston Cup's best dozen.

Nigel Kinrade

13 **Sterling Marlin** - For the second year in a row Marlin's magic on the superspeedways was missing. No wins and no top fives for the driver who finished third in the 1995 standings.

14 **Jimmy Spencer** - An accident at the Brickyard forced Spencer to miss two events in the second half of the season after enjoying a high standing in the first half. Despite the two race handicap he still scored three top fives and eight top tens.

Nigel Kinrade

15 **Chad Little** - Little enjoyed the best year of his career as a new member of the Jack Roush Racing powerhouse. His second place in the Texas 500 was his highest finish ever.

Nigel Kinrade

16 **Ward Burton** - Two 1998 poles attest to Burton's speed and a solid second place at Charlotte in the fall attest to his finishing ability. With better consistency he would have made the year's top ten.

17 **Michael Waltrip** - 1998 was another top twenty year for Waltrip, with five top five finishes. Making the top ten in '99 is the goal, but 12th in 1994 and '95 is the closest Waltrip has come.

18 **Bill Elliott** - NASCAR's "Most Popular Driver," for the 13th time, Elliott has the most loyal fan base in the sport. However, the architect of 40 career victories has been looking for 41 since 1994.

19 **Ernie Irvan** - The fire is still there. Irvan scored three poles in 1998. In the first half, he was on course to a top ten year but had to sit out the last three races with post concussion syndrome.

20 **Johnny Benson** - The 1996 Rookie of the Year had seven top ten finishes in the first 11 races of the year as a Roush Racing driver. A streak of bad luck frustrated his campaign to make the year's top ten.

NASCAR Winston Cup Race 1
Daytona 500
Daytona International Speedway
Daytona Beach, FL
February 15, 1998
200 Laps, 500 Miles

DALE DOES IT, AT LAST, WINS THE DAYTONA 500

On his 20th attempt, Dale Earnhardt nailed down the one prize that had eluded him in a stellar career, studded with seven Winston Cup driver's titles. Even the fact that the last lap was run under caution couldn't detract from his emotional Chevrolet powered trip to victory circle, laden about equally with elation and relief. Although Earnhardt's hard nosed driving style hardly makes him the most popular member of the Winston Cup drivers clan, dozens of crew members lined up on pit lane to congratulate him. Polesitter Bobby Labonte, Pontiac mounted, finished second, opined that he would have had a hard time catching Earnhardt had a Jimmy Spencer-John Andretti tangle not caused the last lap yellow. Jeremy Mayfield finished third in a fine debut drive aboard the new to NASCAR Ford Taurus. The win was Earnhardt's 71st, his first in over a year, and gained him $1,059,105 a record purse for the event. Earnhardt's arch rival Jeff Gordon was victimized by a bent spoiler, finished 16th after leading 56 laps, was not in a position to spoil Earnhardt's big day when the final countdown came.

The top five drivers in the Winston Cup points chase following the Daytona 500 were: Dale Earnhardt, 185, Bobby Labonte, 175, Jeremy Mayfield, 165, Ken Schrader, 160, and Rusty Wallace, 160 points.

Nigel Kin

Nigel Kinrade

NASCAR Winston Cup Race 2
GM Goodwrench 400
North Carolina Motor Speedway
Rockingham, NC
February 22, 1998
393 Laps, 400 Miles

JEFF GORDON REBOUNDS AT ROCKINGHAM, HOLDS OFF A FLOTILLA OF FORDS

Jeff Gordon and Ray Evernham combined driving and engineering skills for a handsome victory at Rockingham's one-mile oval in what could be a harbinger of the long season to follow. Ford drivers Rick Mast and Kenny Wallace were the fastest qualifiers, occupied the front row of the starting grid. At the finish, six of the new Ford Taurus drivers: Rusty Wallace, Mark Martin, Jimmy Spencer, Geoff Bodine, Bill Elliott, and Dale Jarrett chased Gordon across the finish line to no avail. Wallace was 1.28 seconds behind at the finish. What Evernham contributes to the race day game plan is the ability to fine tune the car as the

contest develops. No other Chevrolet team seems to have this talent to the same degree. Certainly not the Dale Earnhardt-Larry McReynolds duo on this occasion. The Daytona 500 winner complained about push, "going into the corners and coming out of them." He finished a lap down.

The top five drivers in Winston Cup points following the Goodwrench 400 were: Rusty Wallace, 335, Dale Earnhardt, 302, Jeff Gordon, 300, Jeremy Mayfield, 291, and Bill Elliott with 289 points.

NASCAR WInston Cup Race 3
Las Vegas 400
Las Vegas Motor Speedway
Las Vegas, NV
March 1, 1998
267 Laps, 400.5 Miles

MARK MARTIN LEADS THE FORD PHALANX AT LAS VEGAS

Mark Martin led a seven car Ford charge across the finish line at Las Vegas, winning his first race of the year and setting off howls of anguish in the Chevrolet camp,

which has been urging NASCAR officials to lower spoiler height on the new Taurus. Not even white knight Jeff Gordon could come to the rescue this time. He finished a lap down in 17th place. First of the Chevrolet pilots was hard campaigner Dale Earnhardt in the eighth slot. To add to the rout, Earnhardt was followed by six more Taurus drivers Bill Elliott, Chad Little, Rick Mast, Ricky Rudd, Geoff Bodine, and Michael Waltrip. Gordon's teammate Terry Labonte, second best of the Chevrolet cadre, netted 15th place.

This kind of dominance by one nameplate does get a response from NASCAR officials. They lowered the Ford's rear spoiler one-quarter inch prior to the next round at Atlanta. Gordon's mechanical guru, Ray Evernham, called the modest downgrade "a joke," saying that a full inch was necessary to make any difference.

The top five drivers after Las Vegas were: Rusty Wallace, 505, Dale Earnhardt, 449, Jeremy Mayfield, 446, Jimmy Spencer, 429, and Bill Elliott, 427 points.

NASCAR Winston Cup Race 4
Primestar 500
Atlanta Motor Speedway
Hampton, GA
March 9, 1998
325 Laps, 500.5 Miles

BOBBY LABONTE LOVES ATLANTA, TAKES SECOND WIN IN A ROW

Bobby Labonte continued his winning ways at Atlanta in a Pontiac Grand Prix, followed by a flock of Ford drivers, eight in all. Dale Jarrett and Jeremy Mayfield led the blue oval contingent ahead of Rusty Wallace, Kenny Irwin, Dick Trickle, Wallace's brother Kenny, Jeff Burton, and Johnny Benson. Somewhat overlooked in the Chevrolet teams' complaints about the Ford advantage, is the fact that NASCAR rules allow the Pontiacs taller rear spoilers and longer front spoilers than either Ford or Chevrolet are permitted. The Pontiac teams seem to have sorted out their chassis problems well enough to take advantage of this edge, an observation borne out by Pontiac mounted John Andretti's capture of the Atlanta pole and his 33 laps in front at the start of the race.

Starting alongside of Andretti on the front row was Todd Bodine in another Pontiac Grand Prix. Bodine finished 10th. Polesitter Andretti got some pit adjustments that took the sharp edge off his Grand Prix and scuttled his chances for victory, had to settle for 20th. Terry Labonte, Dale Earnhardt, and Kevin Lepage were the top Chevrolets with Labonte scoring in 12th position.

After Atlanta, the top five Winston Cup points producers were: Rusty Wallace, 665, Jeremy Mayfield, 616, Dale Earnhardt, 578, Bill Elliott, 557, and Terry Labonte, 526.

NASCAR Winston Cup Race 5
TranSouth Financial 400
Darlington Raceway
Darlington, SC
March 22, 1998
293 Laps,.400 Miles

DALE JARRETT NIPS JEFF GORDON AT DARLINGTON

A mere .228 seconds separated Ford mounted winner Dale Jarrett and Chevrolet ace Jeff Gordon at the finish of Darlington's TranSouth Financial 400. Gordon started back in 24th place and made a valiant, if unsuccessful effort to dislodge Jarrett who led the last eight laps, as well as five other times during the contest. While moving up relentlessly, Gordon never did manage to snare the lead. Ford drivers Mark Martin and Jeff Burton were the fastest qualifiers, with Burton ending up fifth and Martin seventh, Rusty Wallace nailed down third place followed by Jeremy Mayfield. Burton was a particularly strong contender, taking the lead on lap seven and running in front on five other occasions.

39 of the 43 starters were running at the finish and only two, Geoff Bodine and Greg Sacks, were accident victims, both in single car excursions into the wall. Overall, it was a remarkably incident free event on the track "Too Tough To Tame." Jarrett, Mayfield, and Burton were in the thick of the day's action at the front, until Gordon's late charge which fell just short.

Following the TranSouth Financial 400, the top five drivers were: Rusty Wallace, 835, Jeremy Mayfield, 781, Dale Earnhardt, 705, Jeff Gordon, 688, and Bill Elliott with 680 points.

Nigel Kinrade

NASCAR Winston Cup Race 6
Food City 500
Bristol Motor Speedway
Bristol, TN
March 29, 1998
500 Laps, 266.5 Miles

JEFF GORDON LEADS A HENDRICK RACING 1-2 AT BRISTOL

Reinforcing his stature as the driver to beat in the 1998 Winston Cup campaign incumbent champion Jeff Gordon notched his second victory of the year at Bristol, with teammate Terry Labonte just over one half second in arrears at the finish. Gordon was the first driver to score two wins in the unfolding 1998 title chase. It was his fourth early season win at Bristol. His strength in the closing stages afforded hints of more to come. Polesitter Rusty Wallace paced the field for the first two thirds of the race, with third fastest qualifier Labonte in close contention.

Once again Gordon elected to let the leaders come to him. Although starting on the front row, he did not take the point position until lap 438. With Labonte between him and any non-Hendrick challengers his path to the checkered flag was smooth and swift. Dale Jarrett carved out a solid third place to position himself among the year's leading title contenders. Atlanta winner Bobby Labonte was claimed by an accident, managed only 442 laps.

After Bristol, the Winston Cup points leaders were: Rusty Wallace, 909, Jeremy Mayfield, 908, Jeff Gordon, 868, Terry Labonte, 851, and Bill Elliott, 803.

NASCAR Winston Cup Race 7
Texas 500
Texas Motor Speedway
Ft. Worth, TX
April 5, 1998
354 Laps, 500 Miles

MARK MARTIN TAKES THE CRASH MARRED TEXAS 500

For the second year in a row, a multiple car crash in the opening lap of the Texas 500 at Texas Motor Speedway generated criticism of the layout - and a persistent water seepage problem. Ten cars were involved, four damaged too severely to continue. Others like Jeff Gordon and Dale Earnhardt spent most of the day in damage control mode and finished far down the list of starters. For Martin and his Roush Racing Ford mounted teammates, Chad Little and Johnny Benson, it was a banner day; they finished first, second, and fifth in another bit of evidence that multiple car teams are highly effective in NASCAR's ever intensifying competition. While he didn't win, it was the best day of his career for Little, who led on four separate occasions. Polesitter Jeremy Mayfield, also had a winning caliber race going, leading four times, until a cut tire dropped him out of contention. Ford driver Robert Pressley took down third place. Fourth place Joe Nemechek, who qualified second, was the leading Chevrolet driver. After Texas, the Winston Cup points leaders were Rusty Wallace, 1036, Jeremy Mayfield, 1012, Mark Martin, 979, Bill Elliott, 927, and Dale Jarrett, 920.

NASCAR Winston Cup Race 8
Goody's Headache Powder 500
Martinsville Speedway
Martinsville, VA
April 20, 1998
500 Laps, 203 Miles

BOBBY HAMILTON BESTS THE FIELD AT MARTINSVILLE

One of the most under appreciated drivers in the Winston Cup ranks, Bobby Hamilton gained his third career victory, his first for his new team Morgan McClure, on Martinsville's demanding half mile. The 1991 Rookie of the Year posted the other two in the employ of Richard Petty, whose team he left at the end of the '97 season. Hamilton's Chevrolet mounted victory, won from the pole, was doubly satisfying. He proved he could win with different teams and outran arch rival John Andretti, his closest competitor. Andretti, who led twice and as late as lap 437, ran out of fuel in a misguided attempt by his crew to beat Hamilton on an "economy run." He slipped back to 18th place, allowing Ted Musgrave, the day's top Ford driver, who was not among the six drivers to lead a lap, to snare runner-up honors. Dale Jarrett, also driving a Ford Taurus, made up 21 places from his starting position to nail down third place. Dale Earnhardt and Jeff Gordon both managed tours in front, but were not in contention at the end, finishing fourth and eighth.

After Martinsville, the leading Winston Cup campaigners were Rusty Wallace, 1191, Jeremy Mayfield, 1158, Terry Labonte, 1086, Dale Jarrett, 1085, and Jeff Gordon, 1085.

NASCAR Winston Cup Race 9
DieHard 500
Talladega Superspeedway
Talladega, AL
April 26, 1998
188 Laps, 500 Miles

BOBBY LABONTE AND PONTIAC PREVAIL AT TALLADEGA

Bobby Labonte clearly demonstrated just how tough he and his Interstate Batteries Pontiac are on the restrictor plate ruled superspeedways by taking Talladega's DieHard 500 from the pole. Added to his Daytona 500 pole, Labonte is batting 1,000 in qualifying at 1998 events on the big two and a half mile ovals. Older brother Terry, in the Kellogg's Corn Flakes Chevrolet, was a major competitor all day. Two laps from the end, however, Bobby followed by Ford drivers Jimmy Spencer and Dale Jarrett blew by his leading Chevrolet, demoting him to fourth place. Second fastest qualifier Dale Earnhardt was again an accident victim, at a track that has often been unkind to him. Jeff Gordon, in the DuPont Refinishes Chevrolet, managed eight laps in the lead, but had to settle for fifth place. The Ford-Chevrolet tussle continues full tilt with Ford drivers holding down the top two places in the points chase and three of the top five.

After Talladega, the Winston Cup points leaders were Rusty Wallace, 1318, Jeremy Mayfield, 1282, Terry Labonte, 1256, Dale Jarrett, 1255, and Jeff Gordon, 1245.

Nigel Kinrade

NASCAR Winston Cup Race 10
California 500 Presented by NAPA
California Speedway
Fontana, CA
May 3, 1998
250 Laps, 500 Miles

MARK MARTIN THE YEAR'S FIRST THREE RACE WINNER

Always a fierce and front running contender, albeit one who has no coveted Winston Cups on his mantel. Mark Martin put his stamp on the 1998 campaign at California, scoring his third win of the year. Even the convincing win, by a husky for NASCAR margin of 1.287 seconds, over fellow Ford driver Jeremy Mayfield, and running the last 44 laps in the lead didn't make Martin totally happy. He complained that, "Every time I thought we had a decent cushion, another caution would come out." Mayfield, who started alongside polesitter Jeff Gordon on the front row, had a good race, boding well for his best year to date. Gordon led the first 21 laps, was nipped by teammate Terry Labonte for third. Darrell Waltrip had his best finish of the year, taking down fifth place. With the season at the one-third mark, it appears to be shaping up as a tussle between Roush Racing's fleet of Ford drivers and Hendrick Motorsports' two Chevrolet pilots, who between them, have won three of the last four Winston Cup campaigns.

Following the California 500, the Winston Cup points leaders were: Jeremy Mayfield, 1457, Terry Labonte, 1421, Jeff Gordon, 1410, Rusty Wallace, 1384, and Mark Martin, 1334.

NASCAR Winston Cup Race 11
Coca-Cola 600
Charlotte Motor Speedway
Charlotte, NC
May 24, 1998
400 Laps, 600 Miles

JEFF GORDON WINS FROM THE POLE AT CHARLOTTE

It's not easy, but Jeff Gordon just keeps getting better. He posted his third victory of the year at Charlotte. As is often his style, he made no serious attempt to lead at the start, allowing second fastest qualifier Ward Burton, in the MBNA America Pontiac, to have that honor. As the race unfolded, he led for short stints on three occasions but didn't assert himself until he took command for good with ten laps remaining. Rusty Wallace, in his Miller Lite Taurus, was the best of the Ford mounted pursuers, taking the runner-up slot. Bobby Labonte pushed his Interstate Batteries Pontiac out in front of two more Ford pilots, Mark Martin and Dale Jarrett, to capture third place.

The race was a typical Gordon performance, let somebody else, anybody else, lead in the early going, put on some pressure at the mid-point and sail into the lead at the end. So far this game plan seems to be working like a charm.

After the Coca-Cola 600, Jeff Gordon led the Winston Cup points chase with 1590, followed by Jeremy Mayfield, 1563, Rusty Wallace, 1559, Mark Martin, 1504, and Terry Labonte, 1461.

NASCAR Winston Cup Race 12
MBNA Platinum 400
Dover Downs International Speedway
Dover, DE
May 31, 1998
400 Laps, 400 Miles

DALE JARRETT DOES IT AT DOVER

The big news at Dover was that Jeff Gordon didn't win. He led 376 of the 400 laps. In the lead eight laps from the end, his astute handlers elected to bring him in for a splash of fuel which knocked him back to third place, which still pays plenty of points under NASCAR's system. Jarrett scored the win with an assist from better fuel mileage. Jeff Burton, also Ford mounted, slipped into second place. Rusty Wallace, another Ford star, set a new record in qualifying on pole, but an early pit stop and poor fuel mileage combined to take him out of contention. Bobby Labonte, front runner of the Pontiac pack, was the fourth place finisher, while Jeremy Mayfield, an early leader in the Winston Cup title chase, kept his hopes alive by finishing fifth. Jarrett has a record of coming on strong in the campaign's closing stages so that today's win was welcome news indeed, hopefully jump starting a run on the title.

The points leaders following this event were: Jeff Gordon, 1765, Jeremy Mayfield, 1718, Rusty Wallace, 1673, Mark Martin, 1655, and Dale Jarrett, 1635.

NASCAR Winston Cup Race 13
Pontiac Excitement 400
Richmond International Raceway
Richmond, VA
June 6, 1998
400 Laps, 300 Miles

TERRY LABONTE TAKES RICHMOND - UNDER CAUTION

Terry Labonte got his first win of the year but not without some help from the NASCAR officials. In response to a four car accident, they ordered the red flag, halting the race on lap 373 when Dale Jarrett was leading.

Jarrett felt a yellow flag was more in order. When the race was resumed the yellow did come out, for Johnny Benson's crash, just after Labonte had bumped his way past Jarrett on lap 298. Jarrett had no opportunity to bump back into the lead and was understandably upset. Rusty Wallace passed Jarrett under this final yellow, but was moved back to third place in the official standings. This was not Wallace's only incident of the day. According to Jeff Gordon, the pole-sitter, Wallace nudged Gordon's Chevrolet hard enough to induce a spin and subsequent crash that dumped the '97 Winston Cup champion down to the bottom end of the day's results. Ken Schrader and Mark Martin avoided all the mix-ups, to finish fourth and fifth respectively.

Winston Cup leaders after Richmond were Jeremy Mayfield, 1868, Rusty Wallace, 1843, Jeff Gordon, 1822, Mark Martin, 1815, and Dale Jarrett, 1815.

Nigel Kinrade

NASCAR Winston Cup Race 14
Miller Lite 400
Michigan Speedway
Brooklyn, MI
June 14, 1998
200 Laps, 400 Miles

MARTIN GETS HIS FOURTH WIN OF THE YEAR AT MICHIGAN

Jeff Gordon, who put his Chevrolet on the second row of the grid at the start, by mid-race had built up a lead of as much as nine seconds. However, on lap 119, there was a "debris" yellow flag. On fresh tires Mark Martin was a match for Gordon, which he hadn't been earlier, and passed him for the second time on lap 150. Gordon never again got back in the lead, had to make do with third place behind Dale Jarrett. Jarrett was making his second runner-up run in a row. Ford drivers Jeff Burton and Jeremy Mayfield rounded out the top five. The "debris" turned

out to be some foam padding of the type used to encase roll bars, leading to the suspicion that it may have reached the track more through design than accident. Yellows do afford tailenders an excellent opportunity to make up nearly a lap on the leaders, without exerting much effort.

Winston Cup points leaders after the Miller Lite 400 were Jeremy Mayfield, 2023, Jeff Gordon, 1997, Mark Martin, 1995, Dale Jarrett. 1990, and Rusty Wallace, 1955.

NASCAR Winston Cup Race 15
Pocono 500
Pocono Raceway
Long Pond, PA
June 21, 1998
200 Laps, 500 Miles

JEREMY MAYFIELD GETS HIS FIRST WINSTON CUP WIN AT POCONO

Adding impetus to his Winston Cup campaign, Jeremy Mayfield notched his first victory of the year,

and his first ever, at Pocono. Doubly satisfying, he beat his chief rival in the '98 points race, Jeff Gordon to the wire. Gordon was on the pole but, except for a brief stint in front at the start, never again gained the lead. Dale Jarrett, continuing to display both speed and consistency, was scored in third place. He led the race twice, as late as lap 169. Jeff Burton and Mark Martin finished fourth and fifth respectively. For Penske South Racing co-owner Mike Kranefuss it was also a happy victory, his first in 108 starts as a NASCAR car owner. Kranefuss opined that, "It took a long time to put the right people together." Mayfield teammate Rusty Wallace was not so lucky. He started on the front row, had an engine blow after only 37 laps.

Winston Cup points leaders after Pocono were Jeremy Mayfield, 2208, Jeff Gordon, 2172, Dale Jarrett, 2160, Mark Martin, 2155, and Terry Labonte, 2008.

NASCAR Winston Cup Race 16
Save Mart/Kragen 350
Sears Point Raceway
Sonoma, CA
June 28,1998
112 Laps, 218 Miles

JEFF GORDON ROLLS TO SEARS POINT VICTORY

Quite a few of the Winston Cup driving fraternity had trouble mastering the new Bruton Smith era layout at Sears Point Raceway. Not Jeff Gordon. He qualified on the pole, cruised to a 2.748 second cushion over Bobby Hamilton at the finish. Hamilton was overjoyed at his runner-up finish, admitted that he normally needed directions to get around a road circuit. Not so happy was Jerry Nadeau whose extensive road racing experience landed him on the front row in qualifying. He landed his Ford in the scenery after only 13 laps. John Andretti, no stranger to road racing, had a good outing, moving his Pontiac up to third place at the end from a 21st starting slot. Bobby Labonte and Rusty

Wallace rounded out the top five. Jeff Burton crashed hard enough to damage the wall and bring out a caution for repairs to same. Happily, he was uninjured.

Following the Save Mart/Kragen 350 the Winston Cup points leaders were Jeff Gordon, 2357, Jeremy Mayfield, 2317, Mark Martin, 2305, Dale Jarrett, 2283, and Rusty Wallace, 2147.

NASCAR Winston Cup Race 17
Jiffy Lube 300
New Hampshire International Speedway
Loudon, NH
July 12, 1998
300 Laps, 317.4 Miles

JEFF BURTON POSTS HIS FIRST VICTORY OF THE YEAR AT NEW HAMPSHIRE

New Hampshire has been good to Jeff Burton. One of his three 1997 wins took place at the New England mile, and this time he cruised to the winner's circle with a

comfortable 7.439 second edge over teammate Mark Martin, who has four 1998 wins in his résumé. An even better indication of Burton's predominance was the fact that he reeled off the last 83 laps in the lead. In qualifying Ricky Craven made a blazing comeback from the post concussion syndrome he had suffered from his April 1997 practice accident, which forced him to take four months off in '98. The race itself was a let down for Craven. Though starting on the pole, he led briefly at the start, he ended up far down the standings in 29th place, a result attributed to competition rustiness. Craven's Hendrick Motorsports teammate Jeff Gordon qualified alongside him on the front row, was nipped by Mark Martin for second place at the end. Rusty Wallace picked up fourth place and Mike Skinner, in one of his better outings, finished fifth. Dale Earnhardt didn't fare as well, ending up 18th.

The top five Winston Cup points leaders at this point were Jeff Gordon, 2527, Mark Martin, 2475, Dale Jarrett, 2429, Rusty Wallace, 2307, and Bobby Labonte, 2205.

Nigel Kinrade

NASCAR Winston Cup Race 18
Pennsylvania 500
Pocono Raceway
Long Pond, PA
July 26, 1998
200 Laps, 500 Miles

JEFF GORDON GRABS THE PENNSYLVANIA 500 AT POCONO

An on form Jeff Gordon put his stamp on Pocono's second 500 mile race of the year from the front row at the start. He led the last 54 laps and had a comfortable 1.153 second cushion over arch rival Mark Martin at the finish. Polesitter Ward Burton was less fortunate. He was highly competitive through the first two thirds of the race, leading laps 136 through 144 before crashing out on lap 171. Brother Jeff took down third place ahead of Bobby Labonte and Dale Jarrett. Seven time champion Dale Earnhardt, showing sparks of his old form, was feisty and in the thick of things until he faded to seventh place at the end. He led laps 122 through 135 and engaged in a bumping match with eventual winner Gordon. The race was a shining

example of the stellar quality of the Gordon-Ray Evernham relationship. Gordon and his car just kept getting better as the race progressed.

Following the Pennsylvania 500 the Winston Cup points leaders were Jeff Gordon, 2712, Mark Martin, 2650, Dale Jarrett, 2584, Jeremy Mayfield, 2499, and Rusty Wallace, 2462.

NASCAR Winston Cup Race 19
Brickyard 400
Indianapolis Motor Speedway
Indianapolis, IN
August 1, 1998
160 Laps, 400 Miles

JEFF GORDON PICKS UP RACING'S BIGGEST PAYCHECK AT THE BRICKYARD 400

The biggest single day paycheck in motor racing history $1.63 million, including the Winston $1 million bonus, landed in Jeff Gordon's lap with a slight assist from Dale Jarrett's crew. All the leaders agreed post race that Jarrett had the day's fastest car, but his Taurus ran out of gas on lap 80, the halfway mark, while lead-

ing Gordon's Chevrolet by four seconds. Jeff Burton may have had a faster car, too, but a mechanical failure earlier in the race gave him no chance to prove it. Gordon rival Mark Martin claimed second place but fell further behind Gordon in the points chase. Gordon won the inaugural 1994 Brickyard 400 and his second victory was greeted by almost unanimous cheers, which is not always the case. Ernie Irvan took the pole, his second at the Brickyard, and led the first 18 laps. His eventual sixth place finish was a credible effort. Bobby Labonte took his Pontiac to third place ahead of Mike Skinner. Dale Earnhardt qualified well down the list, in 28th place but put in a few laps in the lead, ending up fifth. Gordon ran out the last 23 laps in front. The last two laps were run under caution, but runner-up Martin conceded that he didn't have enough car to challenge Gordon.

After the Brickyard 400 the Winston Cup points leaders were Jeff Gordon, 2897, Mark Martin, · 2825, Dale Jarrett, 2704, Rusty Wallace, 2604, and Jeremy Mayfield, 2536.

NASCAR Winston Cup Race 20
The Bud at the Glen
Watkins Glen International
Watkins Glen, NY
August 9, 1998
90 Laps, 220.5 Miles

JEFF GORDON GOES THREE IN A ROW AT THE GLEN

From superspeedways to a genuine road course, Jeff Gordon makes the transition smoothly and seamlessly. His third Winston Cup win in a row and his sixth of the year was earned at the upstate New York circuit that sparked the U.S. post WWII renaissance of road racing. As usual, there were a few road racing specialists entered to challenge the Winston Cup regulars. This time Canadian Ron Fellows spearheaded the invasion. He qualified second after polesitter Gordon, was running second to leader Gordon when he broke a ring gear on the day's first restart. After lengthy repairs he returned to finish next to last. Another road racer, Tommy Kendall, had qualifying problems, managed to get up only as far as 17th place at the finish. Mark Martin, no slouch at road racing himself, again followed Gordon over the finish line. Next in line at the end, Mike Skinner, Rusty Wallace, and Dale Jarrett. In fact, NASCAR regulars have honed their road racing skills and are no longer prime targets on road circuits.

The Winston Cup points leaders at this stage were Jeff Gordon, 3082, Mark Martin, 3000, Dale Jarrett, 2859, Rusty Wallace, 2769, and Jeremy Mayfield, 2606.

NASCAR Winston Cup Race 21
Pepsi 400 presented by DeVilbiss
Michigan Speedway
Brooklyn, MI
August 16, 1998
200 Laps, 400 Miles

MICHIGAN MAKES IT FOUR IN A ROW FOR JEFF GORDON

For the Winston Cup campaigners it was back to the high banks and for Jeff Gordon it was back to victory circle, for a string of four consecutive wins. Ernie Irvan again demonstrated his qualifying talents at the speedway that nearly claimed his life, starting on the pole and finishing a respectable sixth. Bobby Labonte and his Pontiac, again qualifying well on the big fast tracks, started on the front row and finished 1.826 seconds behind Gordon in second place. Dale Jarrett picked up third place while fourth went to Mark Martin who was a factor right up to the end, leading as late as lap 191. Jeff Burton starting back in the second half of the field moved up smartly to fifth. The race was another example of Gordon and mechanical master Ray Evernham putting together a race winning package. Gordon's two tire last pit stop was just the ticket to get him around Martin and into the lead.

Following the MIchigan event the Winston Cup points leaders were Jeff Gordon, 3262, Mark Martin, 3165, Dale Jarrett, 3029, Rusty Wallace, 2863, and Bobby Labonte, 2839.

Nigel Kinrade

NASCAR Winston Cup Race 22
Goody's Headache Powder 500
Bristol Motor Speedway
Bristol, TN
August 22, 1998
500 Laps, 266.5 Miles

MARK MARTIN
TAKES THE GOODY'S 500

After weeks of looking at Jeff Gordon's tailpipes, Mark Martin, in the Valvoline Cummins Ford, finally turned the tables, winning at Bristol and derailing Gordon's bid for five in a row. The "five" in Gordon's day was fifth place. The win was particularly gratifying to Martin whose father Julian died in a plane crash just two weeks earlier. The results were heavily weighted in favor of Ford. Martin teammate Jeff Burton, in the Exide Batteries Ford, was the runner-up, polesitter Rusty Wallace finished third in the Miller Lite car followed by Dale Jarrett. Gordon was top man among the Chevrolet drivers, followed by Dale Earnhardt and Mike Skinner. Martin amazingly led the last 180 laps of the race enroute to a husky 2.185 second margin of victory.

The Winston Cup points leaders following the Goody's 500 were Jeff Gordon, 3417, Mark Martin, 3350, Dale Jarrett, 3194, Rusty Wallace, 3033, and Bobby Labonte, 2932.

Martin's win cut into Gordon's margin as the points leader and the Taurus driver was followed in the standings by two more Ford drivers. Gordon, almost singlehandedly is upholding Chevrolet's honor.

NASCAR Winston Cup Race 23
Farm Aid on CMT 300
New Hampshire International Speedway
Loudon, NH
August 30, 1998
300 Laps, 317.4 Miles

JEFF GORDON BACK ON TOP,
WINS NEW HAMPSHIRE

Beaten at Bristol, it took Jeff Gordon, in the DuPont Automotive Finishes Chevrolet, only a week to bounce back into victory circle at New Hampshire, this time from the pole. Mark Martin resumed his runner-up role and team owner Jack Roush created a brouhaha by claiming that the Hendrick team was in some way "doctoring" their tires. NASCAR inspections and outside chemical testing of the winning tires failed to come up with anything illegal in the way of chemical additives. The prevailing opinion is that the Gordon-Evernham duo's success is due to skill not skullduggery. John Andretti's polished performance in the STP Pontiac gained him third place, followed by Dale Jarrett in the Quality Care Ford Credit Ford and Jeff Burton in the Exide Batteries Ford. Overshadowing Gordon's win was the cheating accusation, which Gordon felt would serve to motivate Evernham and Co. to even higher levels of achievement.

Following the Farm Aid on CMT 300 the top five Winston Cup points leaders were Jeff Gordon, 3597, Mark Martin, 3530, Dale Jarrett, 3359, Rusty Wallace, 3175, and Bobby Labonte, 3083.

NASCAR Winston Cup Race 24
Pepsi Southern 500
Darlington Raceway
Darlington, SC
September 6, 1998
367 Laps, 500 Miles

JEFF GORDON GRABS DARLINGTON'S $1.3 MILLION REWARD

Jeff Gordon put some eye opening numbers on the scoreboard in the Southern 500. In winning, he took his second $1 million R.J. Reynolds bonus, to add to the winner's $134,855 purse. It was his fourth straight Southern 500 win and his 10th victory of 1998. He's in sight of Richard Petty's modern era record of 13 wins in 1975. Beyond the numbers, Gordon had the pleasure of beating a Roush Racing driver in the late stages. This time the victim was Jeff Burton, who was passed by Gordon with 27 laps to go. Burton had been the race's dominant driver up til that point, piling up more laps in the lead than any other competitor.

Burton was not in his physical prime, having suffered severe bruises in a New Hampshire practice crash and nursing a week long virus. Polesitter Dale Jarrett took down third place. Dale Earnhardt displayed good speed, moving up to fourth place at the end from 18th at the start. Jeremy Mayfield was the last of the top five finishers.

The Winston Cup points leaders after the Pepsi Southern 500 were Jeff Gordon, 3777, Mark Martin, 3578, Dale Jarrett, 3529, Rusty Wallace, 3326, and Bobby Labonte, 3201.

NASCAR Winston Cup Race 25
Exide NASCAR Select Batteries 400
Richmond International Raceway
Richmond, VA
September 12, 1998
400 Laps, 300 Miles

JEFF BURTON EDGES JEFF GORDON AT RICHMOND

Another chapter in the heated rivalry between Hendrick Motor- sports and Roush Racing played out at Richmond with Roush's Jeff Burton in front at the finish. His margin over Hendrick's Jeff Gordon was a mere .015 second at the checker. Burton led 203 laps including the final 39. For the last five, Gordon tried everything in his considerable arsenal to get by, but failed. The racing was clean and exciting, quite removed from the pitside "cheating" claims made by the Roush management two weeks earlier. Burton teammate Mark Martin, locked in battle with Gordon for the points lead, claimed third place. Ken Schrader, who qualified his Chevrolet on the front row put in one of his better recent efforts, finishing fourth, just ahead of John Andretti in a Pontiac. Polesitter Rusty Wallace ran off the first 99 laps in the lead, but faded to seventh at the finish.

Following the Exide NASCAR Select Batteries 400 the Winston Cup points leaders were Jeff Gordon, 3952, Mark Martin, 3748, Dale Jarrett, 3644, Rusty Wallace, 3477, and Jeff Burton, 3298.

Nigel Kinrade

NASCAR Winston Cup Race 26
MBNA Gold 400
Dover Downs International Speedway
Dover, DE
September 20, 1998
400 Laps, 400 Miles

MARK MARTIN TAMES DOVER'S "MONSTER MILE"

Mark Martin toured Dover's Monster Mile like Park Avenue on Sunday, leading all but 20 of the 400 laps, including the last 142. He won from the pole with a comfortable cushion of more than two seconds. For his virtuoso performance Martin put a mere 15 point dent in Jeff Gordon's points lead. Gordon took down runner-up honors as he had the week before. Rusty Wallace, on a hot qualifying streak, started on the front row, led for three short stints but could do no better than fifth at the finish. He's now gone 55 races without a win, a long drought for a driver of his caliber. His teammate Jeremy Mayfield, a winner this year,

seems to be blessed with better luck, moving all the way up from 28th to third at the finish. Bobby Labonte, the Pontiac standard bearer, started fifth, finished fourth. Dale Jarrett's seventh place, coupled with 16th the previous week did little to further his campaign for the title.

The Winston Cup points leaders following the MBNA Gold 400 were Jeff Gordon, 4127, Mark Martin, 3933, Dale Jarrett, 3790, Rusty Wallace, 3637, Jeremy Mayfield, 3419, and Bobby Labonte, 3419.

NASCAR Winston Cup Race 27
NAPA Autocare 500
Martinsville Speedway
Martinsville, VA
September 27, 1998
500 Laps, 263 Miles

RICKY RUDD KEEPS HIS STREAK ALIVE AT MARTINSVILLE

Somehow, somewhere, against the odds, Ricky Rudd had managed to win a race in each of the previous 15 years. At Martinsville, he

stretched his skein, to 16 straight and the odds had never been higher. Rudd is an owner/driver, a difficult assignment. He runs a one car team, another handicap in the current competition. He's 42 years old and fighting 93 degree ambient temperature on a tough half mile track. To top it all his cooling equipment failed. Despite all this, he won and led the last 95 laps to boot. Rudd started on the front row alongside polesitter Ernie Irvan, who executed another of his super fast qualifying runs but ended up eighth. Jeff Gordon netted another runner-up slot and another 170 Winston Cup points, adding to his cushion over third finisher Mark Martin, his chief rival for the championship. Rich Bickle, a graduate of NASCAR's truck racing ranks, had a good day, qualifying and finishing fourth. Jeff Burton rounded out the day's top five.

Winston Cup points leaders after the NAPA Autocare 500 were Jeff Gordon, 4297, Mark Martin, 4098, Dale Jarrett, 3827, Rusty Wallace, 3716, and Bobby Labonte, 3553.

NASCAR Winston Cup Race 28
UAW-GM Quality 500
Charlotte Motor Speedway
Charlotte, NC
October 4, 1998
334 Laps, 500 Miles

MARK MARTIN SHINES AT CHARLOTTE, GAINS ON GORDON IN POINTS CHASE

Not even a broken sewage line, which stopped the race for almost three quarters of an hour, could slow Mark Martin's charge to victory lane at Charlotte. When the race was red flagged for repairs, he had already led 60 of the 94 laps completed and put his stamp on the field. Arch rival Jeff Gordon qualified back in 26th place but carved his way up to lead on four separate tours. His chances of winning dissolved when he incurred a bent spoiler in a lap 204 multi-car tangle triggered by Bobby Labonte. "We were lucky to get back up to fifth," stated Gordon post race. Lucky or not, Gordon saw his point margin over Martin sliced by 30 points. The Burton brothers had another of their intra-family tussles, this time the elder sibling, Ward, in the Pontiac, beat out Jeff, in the Taurus, for the runner-up slot. Bobby Hamilton qualified fifth, finished fourth. Following the UAW-GM Quality 500 the Winston Cup points leaders were Jeff Gordon, 4457, Mark Martin, 4283, Dale Jarrett, 3918, Rusty Wallace, 3801, and Jeff Burton, 3672.

NASCAR Winston Cup Race 29
Winston 500
Talladega Superspeedway
Talladega, AL
October 11, 1998

DALE JARRETT GETS HIS THIRD VICTORY OF THE YEAR AT TALLADEGA

Dale Jarrett again proved that he is a force to be reckoned with in restrictor plate races by taking his third victory of the year, at Talladega, the biggest oval on the tour. Jarrett started third, led the first lap but didn't get out front again until 12 laps from the end. In this closing stage he was under severe pressure from eventual runner-up Jeff Gordon, but never faltered, keeping his Quality Care Ford out in front by a mere .140 second at the finish. Gordon's chief rival, Mark Martin was taken out of contention for race honors - and the championship by a typical "restrictor plate" accident, this one initiated by Ernie Irvan, who spent the night in the hospital for observation. The tangle relegated Martin to 34th place and cost him almost 120 points in his battle with Gordon. Terry Labonte was a beneficiary of the accident and the resulting yellow, claimed third place. Jimmy Spencer and Jeremy Mayfield came from way back at the start to finish fourth and fifth.

After the Winston 500 the Winston Cup points leaders were Jeff Gordon, 4632, Mark Martin, 4344, Dale Jarrett, 4098, Rusty Wallace, 3883, and Jeff Burton, 3806.

Nigel Kinrade

NASCAR Winston Cup Race 30
Pepsi 400
Daytona International Speedway
Daytona Beach, FL
October 17, 1998
160 Laps, 400 Miles

JEFF GORDON GRABS TOP HONORS AT DAYTONA'S PEPSI 400

Postponed from its wild fire plagued July date, postponed a half hour for rain, and run under the Daytona lights for the first time, October's Pepsi 400 was made to order for Jeff Gordon. He ran off the last 37 laps in the lead and easily held off polesitter Bobby Labonte's strong late charge, strong indeed, but too late to dislodge the leader. Mike Skinner had one of the better rides of the day taking third place over Jeremy Mayfield. Rusty Wallace, still winless for the year, but in good form, took down fifth place. Further back, in an uncharacteristic 16th place, was Mark Martin, his championship chances all but vanished with only three races to go. At Daytona,

Rookie Kevin Lepage took on the unfortunate role of triggering the seemingly inevitable multiple car restrictor plate accident. Best of the Roush Racing multi-car roster was Jeff Burton's 13th place. Unless Gordon, Evernham, and Co. do something extremely foolhardy, a third Winston Cup for the charismatic young driver is clearly in view.

Winston Cup points leaders following the Pepsi 400 were Jeff Gordon, 4817, Mark Martin, 4459, Dale Jarrett, 4197, Rusty Wallace, 4043, and Bobby Labonte, 3934.

NASCAR Winston Cup Race 31
Dura Lube/Kmart 500
Phoenix International Raceway
Phoenix, AZ
October 25, 1998
312 Laps, 312 Miles

RUSTY WALLACE WALTZES TO VICTORY AT PHOENIX

Too good to be kept out of victory lane for what seemed to him like

"forever," Rusty Wallace took the Phoenix win, his first of the year, under wraps. He led the last 72 laps of a race shortened to 257 laps by a downpour, and finished under caution. Jeff Gordon might have made a race of it had the event gone its scheduled length, but had to settle for seventh place and will have to wait for at least one more race to wrap up the 1998 title. Runner-up Mark Martin cut 34 points from Gordon's lead but is in a highly precarious position as Gordon's chief challenger. Dale Earnhardt delighted his loyal fans by moving up smartly from 39th at the start to third at the end of the abbreviated event. Jeff Burton in the Exide Batteries Ford and Ted Musgrave in the FirstPlus Financial Ford, finished in fourth and fifth place, helped the blue oval to the day's manufacturer's honors.

After the Dura Lube/Kmart 500 the Winston Cup points leaders were Jeff Gordon, 4963, Mark Martin, 4634, Dale Jarrett, 4264, Rusty Wallace, 4228, and Jeff Burton, 4095.

NASCAR Winston Cup Race 32
AC Delco 400
North Carolina Speedway
Rockingham, NC
November 1, 1998
393 Laps, 400 Miles

JEFF GORDON TAKES THE WINSTON CUP IN STYLE, WINNING AT ROCKINGHAM

Not like 1997 when he "backed in" to the Winston Cup with a conservative 18th place finish in the year's last race, Jeff Gordon won 1998 honors with a clear cut victory at Rockingham, with one more event yet to come. The race played out to a classic Gordon-Evernham script, stay close early on, lead briefly around the midpoint, execute an irresistible power play in the closing stage. The closing stage at Rockingham came 10 laps from the end when Gordon displaced Rusty Wallace for the lead and held on to win. In the process Dale Jarrett got around Wallace for runner-up honors. Mark Martin gave the race his best, qualifying on the pole and finishing fourth. As it had been season long, Martin's best wasn't good enough to derail Gordon. Martin's seven wins and overall consistency would be enough to earn a Winston Cup in most years, but not this time. Jeff Burton was the fifth place finisher. He and teammate Martin can now start thinking about a strategy to derail Gordon, now a three time champion, in '99.

Following the AC Delco 400 the Winston Cup points leaders were Jeff Gordon, 5143, Mark Martin, 4799, Dale Jarrett, 4444, Rusty Wallace, 4398, and Jeff Burton.

NASCAR Winston Cup Race 33
NAPA 500
Atlanta Motor Speedway
Atlanta, GA
November 8, 1998
325 Laps, 500.5 Miles

ALREADY THE CHAMPION, GORDON CLOSES OUT THE SEASON WITH VICTORY AT ATLANTA

If there were any lingering doubts about who was "the man" in 1998, Jeff Gordon erased them with a win in the season ending NAPA 500 at Atlanta. Gordon put on quite a show in the rain shortened event which finished under the lights shortly before midnight, after being stopped twice for the persistent precipitation. Gordon was in eighth place when NASCAR officials informed the field that there would be only 25 laps remaining. Gordon moved smartly to the front but was himself passed by Dale Jarrett. Gordon returned the favor with six laps to go and was unchallenged at the end. Mark Martin, though beaten for the title, performed admirably, collected third place ahead of teammate Jeff Burton. Fifth place Todd Bodine piloted the first Chevrolet after Gordon's winning car. Gordon's victory won the manufacturer's championship for Chevrolet, a feat for which he was almost singlehandedly responsible. It was a virtuoso finish to an incredible year as Gordon's 13th win tied Richard Petty's modern single season record.

The top 10 Winston Cup points producers (final) were Jeff Gordon, 5328, Mark Martin, 4964, Dale Jarrett, 4619, Rusty Wallace, 4501, Jeff Burton, 4415, Bobby Labonte, 4180, Jeremy Mayfield, 4157, Dale Earnhardt, 3928, Terry Labonte, 3901, and Bobby Hamilton, 3786.

NASCAR CRAFTSMAN TRUCK SERIES

Ron Hornaday Becomes the First Two Time Title Winner

Nigel Kinrade

In a thrilling last turn, last lap pass in the year's final event, the Sam's Town 250 at Las Vegas, Ron Hornaday dethroned the 1997 champion, Jack Sprague, and regained the title he first held in 1996. No, Hornaday didn't win the race, Sprague did. However, Hornaday's daring move in the NAPA Brakes Chevrolet gained him the second place he needed to become the series' first two time winner - by the ultra slim margin of three points. Sprague, driver of the GMAC Financial Services Chevrolet, was a gracious loser. "We did all we could, and that was win the race. All in all it's been a very good year." Hornaday, who drives for Dale

Earnhardt's DEI team called his second title, "Unbelievable, I couldn't have had a better day." Over the year he had six wins to five for Sprague. Veteran Joe Ruttman of the Roush Racing stable, winner of a single race, finished third in the season's points total. Another Ford mounted Roush driver, Greg Biffle, took down four poles on his way to the Cintas Rookie of the Year title while finishing eighth in the points, the highest ranking ever for a rookie. The series benefitted from a late July procedural change; normal pit stops replacing the mid-race breaks previously in order. Fourteen different drivers visited victory circle, a high for the series, seven of them first time winners. Ford

driver Tony Raines, fifth in the points, was a three time winner. Stacy Compton, in seventh place for the year, had two victories as did tenth place Mike Bliss. Jay Sauter, fourth in the points total, Jimmy Hensley, sixth for the season, Rick Carelli, Andy Houston, Rick Crawford, Terry Cook, Boris Said, and Dennis Setzer each posted a single win. Hornaday's take of $915,407, a record, lifted his career earnings to $2,442,586. As befits the tour's only two time champion, he is now the leading money winner, displacing Sprague in this key category, too. In their season long tussle at the top, Hornaday and Sprague were never separated by more than 77 points.

Last Lap Champion... **Ron Hornaday** made a thrilling last lap pass in the Las Vegas finale that gained him second place in the race and first place in the points.

Nigel Kinrade

Nigel Kinrade

2 Barely Beaten... **Jack Sprague**, despite winning the year's last race, lost the championship by a mere three points to Hornaday.

3 Solid Third Place... **Joe Ruttman**, in repeating his 1997 placement, was out of the top ten only eight times while winning a single race.

Moving Up... **Jay Sauter** improved his 1997 placement by two spots, scored a single race victory.

5 Triple Race Winner... **Tony Raines**, with three, had the most race victories except for the year's top two, making him a clear candidate for future championship honors.

6 First Time Winner... **Jimmy Hensley**, Richard Petty's driver, scored his first win, a popular one, in three full and one partial season in the NASCAR Craftsman Truck ranks.

Nigel Kinrade

Nigel Kinrade

7 Double Winner... **Stacy Compton** was among the elite quintet who posted more than a single win in the highly competitive 1998 season.

8 Rookie of the Year... **Greg Biffle** was the highest placed ever Cintas Rookie of the Year. He scored four poles and led several races marking him for a future starring role.

9 New to the Top Ten... **Ron Barfield** posted two top five and ten top ten placements enroute to the best of his three years on the circuit. His $268,910 in earnings more than double his first two year total.

10 On Hold... **Mike Bliss** had two 1998 victories and four poles, but a lack of consistency cost him his top five ranking of 1997.

Photos: Nigel Kinrade

Nigel Kinrade

NASCAR Craftsman Truck Series Race 1	NASCAR Craftsman Truck Series Race 2	NASCAR Craftsman Truck Series Race 3
Chevy Trucks Challenge	Florida Dodge Dealers 400	Chevy Trucks 150
Walt Disney World Speedway	Homestead Motorsports Complex	Phoenix International Raceway
Orlando, FL	Homestead, FL	Phoenix, AZ
January 18, 1998	April 4, 1998	April 19, 1998
204 Laps, 1 Mile Oval	167 Laps, 1.5 Mile Oval	150 Laps, 1 Mile Oval

RON HORNADAY HUSTLES TO WIN THE SEASON OPENER

Fittingly driving the NAPA Brakes Chevrolet, Ron Hornaday won the first event of the new season, the Chevy Trucks Challenge at Walt Disney World. He was the beneficiary of a tangle between Mike Wallace and Joe Ruttman who were contesting the lead with only a handful of laps remaining. Ruttman recovered to finish second. Wallace didn't. He finished back in 24th place, eight laps off the pace. Polesitter Chuck Bown had a great first half race. He led the initial 116 laps before giving way to Hornaday who started alongside him on the front row. Rick Carelli took down third place, '97 champion Jack Sprague was fourth and surprising Rookie Greg Biffle of Roush Racing finished fifth in his first 1998 outing.

RICK CRAWFORD RULES AT HOMESTEAD

A 12th place starting position proved only a temporary handicap to Ford driver Rick Crawford who notched his first series win at Homestead. He finished 2.408 seconds in front of runner-up Jack Sprague, in the Team Hendrick Chevrolet, who started on the pole and led the first five laps. The other front row starter, Mike Bliss, in the Team ASE Racing Ford, ended up in 14th place. Jack Sauter, in the GM Goodwrench Service Plus Chevrolet, was third at the end, followed by rapid Rookie Greg Biffle, in the W.W. Grainger Racing Ford, and Ron Barfield driving the Ortho Lawn & Garden Chevrolet. Crawford displaced Barfield from the lead to run off 30 consecutive laps out front enroute to the checker.

RON HORNADAY ON TOP AT PHOENIX

Ron Hornaday, in the NAPA Brakes Chevrolet, became the series' first two time winner at Phoenix at the expense of arch rival Jack Sprague, in the Team Hendrick Chevrolet, the runner-up by 1.464 seconds. After polesitter Stacy Compton, in the Royal Crown Cola Ford, the eventual third place finisher, led the first 37 laps, Sprague and Hornaday swapped the lead five times. Hornaday had the top spot at the end. Rookie Andy Houston, in the Addington Racing Chevrolet, placed fourth with the Homestead winner, Rick Crawford, in the Circle Bar Motel & RV Park Ford, fifth. Hornaday had never before won at Phoenix whereas Sprague had victories at the desert layout in 1996 and 1997.

NASCAR Craftsman Truck Series Race 4
Craftsman 200 by NAPA Auto Parts
Portland Speedway
Portland, OR
April 25, 1998
200 Laps, .5 Mile Oval

STACY COMPTON IN CONTROL AT PORTLAND

From his outside front row starting position Stacy Compton, in the Royal Crown Cola Ford, quickly passed the polesitter and fellow Ford driver Greg Biffle. Compton was unstoppable, led all but two laps of the Craftsman 200 by NAPA Auto Parts. Biffle, in the W.W. Grainger Racing Ford, encountered problems and finished 31 laps off the pace. Randy Tolsma, starting on the second row, had a good outing leading to the runner-up slot. Rick Carelli took down third place. Jack Sprague and Tony Raines rounded out the top five. Ron Hornaday, winner the previous week at Phoenix, had to settle for sixth place today.

NASCAR Craftsman Truck Series Race 5
NAPACARD 200
Evergreen Speedway
Monroe, WA
May 9, 1998
200 Laps, .646 Mile Oval

JACK SPRAGUE EXCELS AT EVERGREEN

Once past polesitter and early leader Joe Ruttman after a 38 lap pursuit, Jack Sprague did a workmanlike job of holding off old rival Ron Hornaday in the closing stages of the NAPACARD 200. Sprague stayed in front for a dominating 161 laps to cop his first 1998 victory by more than two seconds. Ruttman had problems that dropped him a lap down into 12th place at the finish. Randy Tolsma came from 14th on the starting grid to third place at the checker. Rapid Rookie Greg Biffle started on the second row but was two laps down at the end. The season continues to shape up as a Hornaday-Sprague battle.

NASCAR Craftsman Truck Series Race 6
Yellow Freight 200
I-70 Speedway
Odessa, MO
May 23, 1998
200 Laps, .543 Mile Oval

TONY RAINES OWNS ODESSA

Polesitter Tony Raines led the first six and the last 176 laps of the Yellow Freight 200. His Pennzoil Ford was 1.367 seconds ahead of runner-up Joe Ruttman's Exide Batteries Ford at the finish. The other occupant of the front row of the starting grid, Rick Carelli, in the RE/MAX International Chevrolet, was less fortunate, completing only 88 laps. Team ASE Racing Ford driver Mike Bliss and Bryan Reffner, in the Carlin Burners & Controls Ford, were third and fourth at the checker. The year's two points leaders Jack Sprague and Ron Hornaday had another of their typical battles, this time for fifth and sixth place, with Sprague having the edge.

Nigel Kinrade

NASCAR Craftsman Truck Series Race 7
Parts America 150
Watkins Glen International
Watkins Glen, NY
May 30, 1998
65 Laps, 2.45 Mile Road Course

JOE RUTTMAN'S LAST LAP HEROICS LAND HIM IN WATKINS GLEN WINNER'S CIRCLE

Canadian Ron Fellows knows the way around Watkins Glen's challenging road circuit. He's always in demand when NASCAR visits the upstate layout. This time he put the AER Mfg. Chevrolet on the pole. Unfortunately, he didn't lead a single lap and was out after 18. Another "road racer," Boris Said, took the early lead before being displaced by Ron Hornaday who was a factor all afternoon. Hornaday was leading the race with a lap to run when he was passed not only by winner Joe Ruttman, who started on the front row, but Jay Sauter and Said, as well. Hornaday rival Jack Sprague was right behind him in fifth place at the checker.

NASCAR Craftsman Truck Series Race 8
Pronto Auto Parts 400
Texas Motor Speedway
Fort Worth, TX
June 5, 1998
167 Laps, 1.5 Mile Oval

TONY RAINES TAMES TEXAS FOR SECOND WIN OF THE SEASON

Tony Raines, in the Pennzoil Ford, started back in 12th place in the Pronto Auto Parts 400 and didn't work his way to the front until lap 147. Once there, he stayed ahead of Rookie Andy Houston, in the Addington Racing Chevrolet, all the way to the checker, by a .231 second margin. Jack Sprague was on the pole, but finished sixth, still gaining ground over championship rival Ron Hornaday who could do no better than 24th. Joe Ruttman, winner the previous week at Watkins Glen, had another good outing, finishing third. Kevin Harvick, in the Spears Mfg. Chevrolet, and Stacy Compton, in the Royal Crown Cola Ford, took down the last two slots in the top five.

NASCAR Craftsman Truck Series Race 9
Loadhandler 200
Bristol Motor Speedway
Bristol, TN
June 20, 1998
206 Laps, .533 Mile Oval

RON HORNADAY BOUNCES BACK, WINS AT BRISTOL

After an uncharacteristic finish in the bottom half of the field at Texas, Ron Hornaday bounced back to the top, winning Bristol's Loadhandler 200 in style. He set a record in qualifying on the pole at 121.131 mph. Additionally, he had the pleasure of besting prime rival Jack Sprague who became the runner-up. Sprague, in the Team Hendrick Chevrolet, started alongside Hornaday on the front row and the pair traded the lead four times. Hornaday was in charge for the last 133 laps and ahead by .854 second at the checker. Joe Ruttman qualified third, finished the same way. Mike Wallace and Randy Tolsma topped the rest of the field, including Texas winner Tony Raines who was sixth today.

NASCAR Craftsman Truck Series Race 10
Diehard 200
The Milwaukee Mile
West Allis, WI
July 4, 1998
200 Laps, 1 Mile Oval

NASCAR Craftsman Truck Series Race 11
NAPA Autocare 200
Nazareth Speedway
Nazareth, PA
July 11, 1998
200 Laps, 1 Mile Tri-Oval

NASCAR Craftsman Truck Series Race 12
The No Fear Challenge
California Speedway
Fontana, CA
July 18, 1998
100 Laps, 2 Mile Oval

MIKE BLISS BREAKS THROUGH FOR THE WIN AT MILWAUKEE

A four time winner prior to the start of this year's campaign but winless in 1998, Mike Bliss, in the Team ASE Racing Ford, is too good a driver to kept out of victory circle for long. His convincing win from the front starting row included leading the last 49 laps and a husky cushion of 2.181 seconds over runner-up Jimmy Hensley, one of the series' most popular drivers who is still seeking his first victory. Polesitter Jack Sprague led the first 47 laps to notch third place, one slot above season long rival Ron Hornaday, winner of the previous round at Bristol. Outstand-ing newcomer Greg Biffle added strength to his Rookie of the Year campaign with a workmanlike fifth place finish from 17th starting position in the W.W.Grainger Racing Ford.

RON HORNADAY NOTCHES TOP HONORS AT NAZARETH

Although record setting polesitter Mike Bliss led twice in the early going, with a stint by Kevin Harvick in between, he encountered problems which dropped him to 25th place, 45 laps off the pace. Ron Hornaday, in the NAPA Brakes Chevrolet, picked up the lead and breezed through the final 143 laps essentially unchallenged. He was almost four seconds ahead of runner-up Stacy Compton, in the Royal Crown Cola Ford, at the finish. Rival Jack Sprague, in the Team Hendrick Chevrolet, lost ground in their ongoing battle for the championship with a tenth place finish. Rick Crawford, the other front row starter, in the Circle Bar Motel & RV Ford, had even poorer luck. He failed to make it to the halfway mark. Jay Sauter, Butch Miller, and Joe Ruttman completed the top five.

JACK SPRAGUE SOARS AT CALIFORNIA

Rookie Andy Houston was in no way intimidated by the ultra fast California layout, qualifying on the pole at over 172 mph and finishing a creditable fourth. Jack Sprague edged not only arch rival Ron Hornaday for top honors, but Winston Cup regular Ernie Irvan as well. Irvan in turn edged Hornaday for the runner-up slot. The race played out as another Sprague-Hornaday seesaw, with Sprague in front when it counted. Sprague was in command for the last 12 laps and posted a slim .364 second margin over a hard charging Irvan at the end. Mike Skinner, in a rare series appearance, took down fifth place. The race average speed was 141.844 mph, a remarkable number in view of the trucks' less than ideal aerodynamics for high speed ovals.

Nigel Kinrade

NASCAR Craftsman Truck Series Race 13
Tempus Resorts 300K
Pikes Peak International Raceway
Fontain, CO
July 25, 1998
198 Laps, 1 Mile Oval

RON HORNADAY ON TOP AT PIKES PEAK

No Hornaday-Sprague lead swapping drama this time. Pikes Peak was all Hornaday. He won in convincing fashion, reeling off the last 45 laps in front, in the NAPA Brakes Chevrolet. He led Tony Raines, in the Pennzoil Ford, to the checker by .986 second. Sprague finished way back in 31st place, losing considerable ground to Hornaday in their tussle for the title. Mike Bliss, in the Team ASE Racing Ford, set another record in claiming the pole at an average speed of 132.402 mph. He ended up sixth at the end. Third place went to Joe Ruttman. Rick Carelli and Jimmy Hensley completed the top five. Road racing specialist Ron Fellows had no luck on the oval, completing only 18 laps.

NASCAR Craftsman Truck Series Race 14
Cummins 200 by Dodge
Indianapolis Raceway Park
Claremont, IN
July 20, 1998
200 Laps, .686 Mile Oval

JACK SPRAGUE SCORES AT INDIANAPOLIS RACEWAY PARK

In a reversal of last week's results, Sprague took the GMAC Chevrolet to the top of the charts at Indianapolis Raceway Park, and arch rival Ron Hornaday, the winner at Pikes Peak, ended up near the bottom in his NAPA Brakes Chevrolet. Sprague, in the GMAC Financial Services Chevrolet, had a generous margin of more than two seconds over the surprise runner-up, Tony Roper, in the Icehouse Beer Ford. Joe Ruttman scored third place and its useful points payoff. Tony Raines, in the Pennzoil Ford, placed fourth while Lonnie Rush brought the Ohio State University Chevrolet home fifth. Polesitter Randy Tolsma, in the IWX Motor Freight Chevrolet, had to settle for sixth place at the checker.

NASCAR Craftsman Truck Series Race 15
Pennzoil/VIP Discount Tripleheader
New Hampshire International Speedway
Loudon, NH
August 2, 1998
200 Laps, 1.058 Mile Oval

ROOKIE ANDY HOUSTON'S LAST LAP PASS EARNS TOP HONORS AT NEW HAMPSHIRE

An audacious pair of rookies, Andy Houston and Greg Biffle, stole the show at New Hampshire. They swapped the lead three times with Houston's last lap pass of Biffle the decisive one. Jack Sprague and Ron Hornaday, the series' usual providers of this brand of theatrics had more sedate outings, finishing eighth and tenth respectively. Consistent Joe Ruttman scored his third third place in a row with Ron Barfield and Tony Raines completing the top five. Houston and Biffle are in close contention for the coveted Cintas Rookie of the Year title, putting on a freshman version of the Hornaday-Sprague struggle at the championship level.

NASCAR Craftsman Truck Series Race 16
Stevens Beil/Genuine Car Parts 200
Flemington Speedway
Flemington, NJ
August 8, 1998
200 Laps, .625 Mile Oval

NASCAR Craftsman Truck Series Race 17
Federated Auto Parts 250
Nashville Speedway USA
Nashville, TN
August 15, 1998
250 Laps, .596 Mile Oval

NASCAR Craftsman Truck Series Race 18
Lund Look 275K
Heartland Park Topeka
Topeka, KS
August 23, 1998
81 Laps, 2.1 Mile Road Course

FIRST TIME WINNER TERRY COOK TAKES FLEMINGTON HONORS

Close before, but never previously a winner, Terry Cook took his cherished first ride to the series victory circle at Flemington. Polesitter Stacy Compton appeared to have the race wrapped up, running off the first 166 laps in the lead, while beating off a series of challengers. He ran afoul of the first turn wall on lap 177, handing the lead and the race to Cook, who started fourth. Ron Hornaday claimed the runner-up slot, while rival Jack Sprague had his turn in the basement, with only 63 laps completed. Bryan Reffner scored a solid third place. No third place for Joe Ruttman this time, he ended up one notch down, in fourth. Jimmy Hensley was the fifth man in the top five.

JIMMY HENSLEY HOME FIRST AT NASHVILLE

It was a big day for Richard Petty's popular driver, Jimmy Hensley, his first win in four years on the NASCAR Craftsman Truck Series. It was a big day for Dodge, too, the first 1998 win for the marque. Hensley's win was all the more remarkable, since he started 30th in the Cummins Engine Company Dodge. He had a 35 lap stint in front starting on lap 165 and took over for good on lap 214, running out the last 36 tours for a .540 second margin of victory over runner-up Tony Raines. Rick Crawford, Greg Biffle, who started on the front row, and Mike Wallace completed the top five. It was not a banner day for the series leaders. Ron Hornaday finished seventh, Jack Sprague eleventh.

STACY COMPTON COMES OUT ON TOP AT TOPEKA

Stacy Compton's qualifying skills weren't on display at Topeka, but more importantly his finishing stamina was. From eighth on the starting grid he worked his way into the lead on lap 75 and rolled to a .892 second edge over runner-up Terry Cook, the Flemington winner, at the checker. Boris Said, whose road racing talents were particularly suited to the circuit, was on the pole, but fell back to 22nd place at the checker. Jimmy Hensley, the Nashville winner, again had a strong outing, posting a solid third place. Jack Sprague, the fourth place finisher, gained a few points over eighth place Ron Hornaday in their title struggle. Kevin Harvick was the fifth and final member of the day's top five club.

Nigel Kinrade

Nigel Kinrade

NASCAR Craftsman Truck Series Race 19
Kroger 225
Louisville Motor Speedway
Louisville, KY
August 29, 1998
225 Laps, .438 Mile Oval

TONY RAINES RULES AT LOUISVILLE

Tony Raines, in the Pennzoil Ford, joined the select ranks of multiple race winners in a late race surge at Louisville. Mike Bliss appeared to have the win in hand. He took over from polesitter Terry Cook on lap nine and stayed on top for the next 206 tours. Raines surged by Bliss on lap 216 and piled on a 1.285 second margin of victory in the nine laps remaining. Bliss salvaged runner-up honors and rapid Rookie Andy Houston copped third place. Rival Rookie of the Year candidate Greg Biffle checked in in eighth place. Stacy Compton was the fourth place finisher ahead of Cook who was relegated to fifth at the checker. Jack Sprague in ninth place and Ron Hornaday in 17th had unremarkable outings.

NASCAR Craftsman Truck Series Race 20
Virginia is for Lovers 200
Richmond International Raceway
Richmond, VA
September 10, 1998
200 Laps, .750 Mile Oval

JACK SPRAGUE SPRINGS BACK INTO WINNER'S CIRCLE AT RICHMOND

Jack Sprague, in the GMAC Financial Services Chevrolet, rebounded from his recent run of uninspired outings with a decisive win at Richmond, beating Winston Cup regular Ernie Irvan's Federated Auto Parts Ford in the bargain. Rival Ron Hornaday was again mired in a lowly finish, 22nd. Irvan had 41 laps in front before bowing to Sprague on lap 179 and settling for second place. Remarkable Rookie Greg Biffle, in the W.W. Grainger Ford, was the third place finisher. Steady Joe Ruttman, the polesitter, in the Exide Batteries Ford, ran off another "top five," this time in fourth place. Butch Miller, in the DANA Corporation Dodge, was the fifth of the day's five leading finishers.

NASCAR Craftsman Truck Series Race 21
Memphis 200
Memphis Motorsports Park
Memphis, TN
September 13, 1998
200 Laps, .750 Mile Oval

RON HORNADAY RETURNS TO THE WINNER'S CIRCLE IN MEMPHIS

If Jack Sprague won last week, as he did at Richmond, it's a reasonable bet that Ron Hornaday will counter with a win this week. He did just that at Memphis, in dominating fashion, running in front of the pack for the final 41 laps. Greg Biffle had all the appearances of a winner, leading the first 109 laps from the pole. Unfortunately, it was not to be; 22nd place, four laps down, was his fate at the checker. Jay Sauter scored a handsome second place, with Jimmy Hensley, in good form, arriving third at the checker. Joe Ruttman and Rick Crawford rounded out the top five. Hornaday rival Jack Sprague finished ninth today, losing ground to his number one opponent in the title campaign.

NASCAR Craftsman Truck Series Race 22
Ram Tough 200
Gateway International Raceway
Madison, IL
September 19, 1998
160 Laps, 1.25 Mile Oval

RICK CARELLI CAPTURES GATEWAY'S RAM TOUGH 200

Rick Carelli had threatened before; this time he carried out his threat, winning Gateway's Ram Tough 200 in style by passing leader Jay Sauter with nine laps to go. Carelli's pass, in the RE/MAX International Chevrolet, allowed Ron Hornaday to get by as well, earning runner-up status for Hornaday and demoting Sauter to third place. Greg Biffle scored another pole, a fine effort that went for naught, netting 19th place at the checker. Even that was better than the 30th place finish of Rookie of the Year rival Andy Houston. Jack Sprague, not wanting to lose sight of Hornaday, took down fourth after two sessions at the front of the field. Tom Hubert finished fifth. Carelli's margin of victory was .351 second. Jimmy Hensley, in sixth place, was the top Dodge driver.

NASCAR Craftsman Truck Series Race 23
NAPA 250
Martinsville Speedway
Martinsville, VA
September 26, 1998
250 Laps, .525 Mile Oval

JAY SAUTER SPEEDS TO VICTORY AT MARTINSVILLE

A winner in 1997, Jay Sauter, in the GM Goodwrench Service Plus Chevrolet, became a 1998 winner in Martinsville's NAPA 250 by passing race leader Ron Hornaday in a late race matchup on lap 236. Jimmy Hensley got by Hornaday, too, for the runner-up slot, pushing Hornaday, in the NAPA Brakes Chevrolet, back to third at the checker. No longer surprising, Greg Biffle has established himself as one of the series' quickest qualifiers. He was on the pole again, in the W.W. Grainger Ford, failed to carry his speed to victory circle. Eighth place was his lot today. Stacy Compton cornered fourth place, with fifth going to Rich Bickle. Jack Sprague made the top ten, barely, lost ground to Hornaday in the title chase, with the season running down.

NASCAR Craftsman Truck Series Race 24
Kragen/Exide 151
Sears Point Raceway
Sonoma, CA
October 11, 1998
77 Laps, 1.949 Mile Road Course

ROAD RACER BORIS SAID SCORES AT SEARS POINT

Boris Said put his road racing skills to good use at Sears Point, scoring his first victory of the series. He started alongside polesitter Tom Hubert, with whom he swapped the lead five times. The only other driver to get a nose in front was Rick Carelli, and then only for a single lap. Hubert lasted only 54 laps. Unchallenged, Said had a huge lead of more than six seconds at the finish over second place Mike Bliss. Tony Raines, Joe Ruttman, and Jimmy Hensley were even further behind, while rounding out the top five. The series' top pair, Jack Sprague and Ron Hornaday, did not fare well on the road course, Sprague was ninth, Hornaday 23rd. They can look forward to better days, all three of the remaining events are on ovals.

Nigel Kinrade

NASCAR Craftsman Truck Series Race 25
Dodge California Truck Stop 300
Mesa Marin Raceway
Bakersfield, CA
October 18, 1998
300 Laps, .5 Mile Oval

DENNIS SETZER SETS THE PACE AT MESA MARIN

Dennis Setzer performed a neat trick at Mesa Marin, winning the Dodge California 300 in the Mopar Performance Dodge, the second victory of the year for the marque and Setzer's first ever. In three years on the circuit Setzer had only previously been in the top five once, so the victory merited a special celebration. Setzer started back in 12th place and got to the front only once, for the final ten laps. Ron Hornaday, in the NAPA Brakes Chevrolet, started on the pole, but finished fourth. He was outrun by rival Jack Sprague, who moved up to the runner-up slot from tenth on the starting grid in the GMAC Financial Services Chevrolet. Stacy Compton, the other occupant of the front row at the start, finished third in the Royal Crown Cola Ford, with Kevin Harvick, in the Spears Mfg. Chevrolet, the final member of the top five club.

NASCAR Craftsman Truck Series Race 26
GM Goodwrench Service Plus/AC Delco 300
Phoenix International Raceway
Phoenix, AZ
October 24, 1998
186 Laps, 1 Mile Oval

MIKE BLISS WINS FROM THE POLE AT PHOENIX

Mike Bliss captured the pole and top race honors at Phoenix with a convincing turn of speed that allowed him to lead the final 53 laps relatively pressure free in his Team ASE Racing Ford. He was almost three seconds ahead of runner-up Greg Biffle, in the W.W. Grainger Ford, at the checker. Ron Hornaday's third place, in the NAPA Brakes Chevrolet, was good enough to gain him the points lead over Jack Sprague whose unlucky 13th place finish was attributable to carburetor problems in his GMAC Financial Services Chevrolet. Joe Ruttman, in the Exide Batteries Ford, and Andy Houston, in the Addington Racing Chevrolet, were the other two top five finishers. With today's misfortune, Sprague will have to win the year's finale in Las Vegas and Hornaday finish no better than third to capture the crown.

NASCAR Craftsman Truck Series Race 27
Sam's Town 250 by Las Vegas Events
Las Vegas Motor Speedway
Las Vegas, NV
November 8, 1998
169 Laps, 1.5 Mile Oval

JACK SPRAGUE WINS A THRILLING SAM'S TOWN 250, LOSES THE TITLE TO RUNNER-UP RON HORNADAY

In a gaming city, Jack Sprague knew he'd have to win the Sam's Town 250 to have any chance at the series championship. He did, with a picture perfect pass of Greg Biffle one lap from the end. Points leader Ron Hornaday knew he'd have to take second place to clinch the title. He did, with an equally thrilling last lap pass of Biffle and Joe Ruttman. It was a fitting finish to an exciting season's rivalry, matched only in its intensity by its good sportsmanship. Jimmy Hensley and Jay Sauter also got past Biffle, who finished fifth. Sprague not only won the race, he was the polesitter as well. However, his sterling performance couldn't ward off Hornaday's fine run. Hornaday's points leadership position going into the event, plus second place in the race, was just enough to earn him the championship.

PEP BOYS INDY RACING LEAGUE

A.J. Foyt Fields Champion Kenny Brack in a Year of Progres.

More entries, more races, fewer injuries and a major series sponsor who put up a $1 million bonus for the first champion under its banner marked the substantial progress made by the Indy Racing League in 1998, its third year, the second of its four liter normally aspirated engine formula. That the big bonus was claimed by a Swedish driver, Kenny Brack, fielded by four time Indianapolis 500 winner A.J. Foyt, one of the biggest backers of the IRL and its policy of developing young American oval track stars, is a testament to Foyt's skill in evaluating drivers - and somewhat ironic. In addition to being Swedish, Brack had virtually no oval track experience prior to his IRL rookie year of 1997. Not a standout in qualifying, Brack was a polished finisher, winning three times, more than any other driver. This latter quality endeared him to Foyt as did Brack's winning total of 332 points. Foyt's number one driver of '97, American Davey Hamilton, who finished second in that year's title chase, but was not resigned, finished second again in '98, this time for Nienhouse Racing. Hamilton's runner-up spot was secured without winning a race but by scoring 292 points on consistency.

Another young American star, Tony Stewart, the '97 IRL titleholder, retained his remarkable turn of speed but failed to match his year earlier pace and settled for third in the title chase with two victories and 289 points. He's off to a promising career in NASCAR's Winston Cup,

with its more substantial financial rewards in '99, but would love to come back for the Indianapolis 500 - and its big payday despite being booked for a NASCAR race the same day. The two races in one day assignment is difficult but doable. Brilliant on occasions, Scott Sharp also notched two victories, along the route to 272 points and fourth place for the year. Buddy Lazier, the hero of the 1996 Indy 500, was consistent but not victorious. His 262 points notched fifth place for the season.

The Indianapolis 500 winner was car owner/driver Eddie Cheever, who kept the lion's share of the big winner's check at home. He just made the year's top ten, ninth for the year with 222 points. Billy Boat, Foyt's other driver, was a talented qualifier, on the pole in six of the 11 events, and raising eyebrows in the pits at his speed differential over the rest of the field. This despite missing two races with a broken leg incurred in a New Hampshire accident. He won at Texas but failed to make the podium in his last four starts despite claiming the pole in all of them. His 194 points were good only for 13th place.

John Paul Jr. got a long awaited and very popular victory in the second Texas outing of the year, but missed the top ten with 216 points.

Veteran Arie Luyendyk closed out his season by winning the Las Vegas finale, which helped him into top ten territory for the year, eighth place and 227 points. He's contemplating retirement in '99 but could probably be tempted to try for a third

Indianapolis 500 win in 1999.

Rookie of the Year Robby Unser, son of three time Indianapolis 500 winner Bobby Unser, had a good outing in the 1998 500, finishing fifth. He scored 176 points in eight races for Cheever's team.

In terms of the IRL's progress, Foyt put it this way. "It's a lot further along than I expected."

On the equipment front, Oldsmobile, Dallara, and Goodyear walked off with the year's honors. Olds Aurora engines continued their unbeaten string, having won every race run under IRL's current four liter formula. High watermark for Nissan's Infinity was 23 leading laps and fourth place for Roberto Guerrero at Texas' second race but Infinity is believed to have signed some new teams for '99. Dallara displaced G-Force, the 1997 champion, as the winningest chassis 8 to 3. Dallara's eight included the crown jewel Indianapolis 500. In a switch on the tire front, Goodyear claimed seven wins to four for Firestone. Goodyears were also on Eddie Cheever's Indianapolis 500 winning car, its first victory in the classic since 1995. Four of Goodyear's seven were chalked up by the forces of team owner A.J. Foyt, a long term Goodyear loyalist. Several additional engine manufacturers have shown interest in the series, but have expressed reservations about IRL's requirement that the engines be available for sale, rather than lease, which better protects proprietary information.

Richard Dole

I Teamwork on Top... **Kenny Brack** (left) of Sweden combined his on-track skills with the encyclopedic car preparation and strategy smarts of car owner A.J. Foyt for a title winning campaign, including three consecutive victories. At Pikes Peak, Brack beat 1997 Champion Tony Stewart and Menard teammate Robbie Buhl (right). Brack scored 332 IRL points.

2 New Team, Same Placement... **Davey Hamilton** moved to Nienhouse Racing from the A.J. Foyt stable was again the runner-up, again without a win. (292 IRL points)

3 Off to NASCAR... **Tony Stewart** was again the man to beat in IRL. The 1997 champion failed to repeat, despite two victories and three poles. (289 IRL points)

4 Brilliant on Occasions... **Scott Sharp** scored two first half victories, but no second half podiums took him out of title contention. (272 IRL points)

5 1996 Indy 500 Hero... **Buddy Lazier** was short of victory lane but consistency earned him top five ranking. (262 IRL points)

Finale Winner... **Arie Luyendyk**, after struggling all year, was victorious in the last race of the season at Las Vegas. (227 IRL points)

Popular Winner... **John Paul Jr.** enjoyed his first trip to the winner's circle, since 1983, at the Lone Star 500 in 1998. (216 IRL points)

Cheryl Day Anderson

Quick in Qualifying... **Billy Boat** qualified for the pole in six of the nine races he drove in, missed out on the winner's circle. (194 IRL points)

Rookie of the Year... **Robby Unser** finished in fifth place at the Indianapolis 500. (176 IRL points)

Cheryl Day Anderson

Pep Boys Indy Racing League Race 1
Indy 200
Walt Disney World Speedway
Lake Buena Vista, FL
January 14, 1998
200 Laps, 200 Miles

FAST START FOR TONY STEWART IN HIS IRL TITLE DEFENSE. HE TAKES DISNEY WORLD OPENER.

He had come close before; second in his first outing at the 1996 Walt Disney World inaugural, a near miss in '97 when an oil line broke while he was in command as the late race leader. The third time was the charm for Tony Stewart. Luck went his way, when race leader Mark Dismore had to pit with only a handful of laps remaining. Stewart ran out the four laps remaining with a husky 8.579 second cushion over runner-up Jeff Ward at the checker. Stewart led the early going from the pole but would have had his hands full trying to get by Dismore, had not the latter been forced to pit for fuel. Davey Hamilton, the runner-up in the 1997 championship, finished third, ahead of Stephan Gregoire and Dismore, whose late pit stop cost him four places. Gregoire might have been the runner-up except that he ran out of fuel, as a result of foregoing a third pit stop. A.J. Foyt's new driver, Kenny Brack, had an inauspicious start, through no fault of his own; a broken suspension part put him more than 20 laps down. If the season opener is any indication, Stewart is amply prepared to take on the challenges of a winning repeat title.

Pep Boys Indy Racing League Race 2
Duralube 200
Phoenix International Raceway
Phoenix, AZ
March 22, 1998
200 Laps, 200 Miles

SCOTT SHARP SCORES AT PHOENIX. TEAMMATE MARK DISMORE GETS THE ASSIST.

Scott Sharp was leading on the final restart with three laps to go, as he had for the previous 26, after taking over the point from Tony Stewart, who retained second place. Stewart was naturally anxious to make a run on Sharp in the final countdown. Only one problem; Sharp teammate Mark Dismore, 25 laps down and out of contention, was between Stewart and his target, Scott. Stewart never really got his shot at Scott and afterward maintained that Dismore had gone so slowly on the restart that Stewart almost stalled. Third place Billy Boat agreed. The officials didn't. Scott was declared the winner, by 2.366 seconds. Stewart was a thoroughly disgruntled runner-up. To add to the controversy, Stewart's managers also claimed that Scott's fuel tank was too large and the differential accounted for the winner's ability to complete the race on two fuel stops, while most of the contenders made three. Polesitter Jeff Ward finished fifth, just behind fourth place Stephan Gregoire. The day's big item was the Dismore-Stewart controversy. As Dismore, a long time friend of Stewart's maintained, "He'll get over it."

Pep Boys Indy Racing League Race 3
Indianapolis 500
Indianapolis Motor Speedway
Indianapolis, IN
May 24, 1998
200 Laps, 500 Miles

EDDIE CHEEVER FINALLY WINS A BIG ONE, THE 82nd INDIANAPOLIS 500

In two decades on the major motorsports scene, encompassing Formula One, CART, and now the Indy Racing League, Eddie Cheever had only one victory in his log book prior to the 1998 Indianapolis 500, the Disney World opening event in IRL's first year. Today, he wrote his name in racing's record book in indelible fashion by winning the Indianapolis 500. With the victory came the usual $1 million-plus purse, a handy item since owner/driver Cheever's team was running on financial fumes. Cheever earned the victory. He had the strongest car over the last 100 miles of the long race and successfully frustrated repeated attempts by runner-up Buddy Lazier, the 1996 winner, to dislodge him from the lead, except for a couple of laps on pit stops. Lazier, as game as ever, was 3.191 seconds behind Cheever at the checker. Steve Knapp took down third place, with Davey Hamilton fourth. Robby Unser, son of three time Indy 500 winner Bobby, added frosting to Cheever's cake by finishing fifth in Cheever's second car and gathering Rookie of the Race honors.

Photos: Richard Dole

Pep Boys Indy Racing League Race 4
True Value 500K
Texas Motor Speedway
Fort Worth, TX
June 6, 1998
208 Laps, 312 Miles

BILLY BOAT THE OFFICIAL WINNER AT TEXAS THIS TIME

Last year at this time Billy Boat thought he had won this race. He made the trip to victory circle to receive the winner's laurels, only to have them snatched away when the then sanctioning group, the U.S. Auto Club, did a review of the lap count. The official 1997 winner, Arie Luyendyk, was not even close this time, finishing 13th, 30 laps down. Nor was polesitter Tony Stewart, with whom Boat swapped the lead repeatedly in the race's midsection. Stewart had a radiator leak that put him out. An inspired Greg Ray came from a midpack starting position to claim the runner-up spot at the checker, battling Boat down to the wire. In a big day for the A.J. Foyt forces, Boat teammate Kenny Brack joined him on the podium with a fine third place. A pair of Scotts, Goodyear and Sharp, collected fourth and fifth place respectively. The day's big happening was the vindication of Boat and car owner Foyt who, in 1997, "nudged" Luyendyk in a victory circle brouhaha over the scoring mix up. Foyt later apologized and was delighted to have an uncontested win this time around.

Pep Boys Indy Racing League Race 5
New England 200
New Hampshire International Speedway
Loudon, NH
June 28, 1998
200 Laps, 212 Miles

TONY STEWART NOTCHES NEW HAMPSHIRE VICTORY

Wanting to exit the IRL on the high ground of a repeat championship, NASCAR-bound Tony Stewart took another big step in that direction with his victory at New England. It was his second win of the year and made him the season's only multiple winner to date. Billy Boat, the year's best qualifier, was on the pole again but had the misfortune to be the victim of an accident not of his making. Raul Boesel hit him amidships when he spun trying to avoid a J.J. Yeley-Donnie Beechler tangle. Boat would be out for two to three races with a broken femur. Those swift Scotts, Goodyear and Sharp, were again podium bound, this time in second and third. Winner Stewart enjoyed a 1.788 second cushion at the checker. Consistent Davey Hamilton checked in in fourth place, while veteran Arie Luyendyk took down fifth, his best result of the year. Post-race he reported. "I'm not happy with a fifth place finish but its better than not finishing." "Not finishing" had been his fate too often this year. Stewart's win vaulted him to the head of the class in the IRL points parade, 167 to 150 for a consistent but winless Scott Sharp.

Pep Boys Indy Racing League Race 6
Pep Boys 400
Dover Downs International Speedway
Dover, DE
July 19, 1998
248 Laps, 200 Miles

SCOTT SHARP MASTERS THE "MONSTER MILE" AT DOVER

Tony Stewart was on the pole again but after Dover's Monster Mile with its 24° banking had taken its toll, Scott Sharp was in command. Sharp led all 45 laps preceding the checker. He passed leader Stewart on lap 162 and was never seriously threatened, although Buddy Lazier was out front for six laps on pit stop maneuvering. There were six "incidents" and seven caution periods, adding up to almost 100 laps of the scheduled 248 being run under yellow. A rare mechanical malady slowed Stewart, a loose dashboard. Then a broken halfshaft, though repaired, knocked him out of contention. Buddy Lazier again made a late race run, again came up short, scoring another runner-up finish, the only other driver on the same lap as the winner. Third place Marco Greco and fourth place Davey Hamilton both were two laps down at the finish, a measure of the attrition on the track. Fifth place Stephan Gregoire was two laps further back of this pair.

Not only did Sharp win a difficult race, he displaced Stewart as the year's points leader 202 to 194.

Pep Boys Indy Racing League Race 7
VisionAire 500
Charlotte Motor Speedway
Charlotte, NC
July 25, 1998
208 Laps, 312 Miles

KENNY BRACK TAKES HIS FIRST IRL WIN AT CHARLOTTE DESPITE PIT STOP MISCUES

Car owner A.J. Foyt said it best, of his driver Kenny Brack's Charlotte win, "I've never seen a crew make so many mistakes and still end up winning." These included a botched tire replacement and mistiming a pit stop. Pole winner Tony Stewart was snakebitten for the second race in a row. This time it was a broken oil line that led to engine failure after only 54 laps. One thing Foyt's crew did right was to give Brack four fresh tires on his last pit stop enabling him to chase down the leaders in the final countdown and finish 5.602 seconds ahead of runner-up Jeff Ward at the finish. Only one Scott, Goodyear, made the podium, in third place. Arie Luyendyk and Marco Greco completed the top five. Greg Ray, subbing for injured Billy Boat for the Foyt forces, performed admirably, qualifying second and leading the early going before transmission troubles took him out.

Points leader Scott Sharp held onto his lead over Stewart 214 to 206 despite banging the wall on lap 105. An indication of the night's proceedings under the lights was that there were three separate mishaps on the first three pace laps before the race actually got underway, a lost nose cone, a fire, and a spin.

Pep Boys Indy Racing League Race 8
Radisson 200
Pikes Peak International Raceway
Fountain, CO
August 16, 1998
200 Laps, 200 Miles

KENNY BRACK MAKES IT TWO IN A ROW AT PIKES PEAK

A.J. Foyt's investment in Swedish driver Kenny Brack, considered a risky one by his fellow team owners prior to the season's start, started

paying real dividends at Pikes Peak. Brack not only won his second race in a row, but beat the rival Team Menard pair of Robbie Buhl and Tony Stewart in the bargain. Brack was 7.542 seconds ahead of runner-up Buhl at the finish. Current champion Stewart finished third. Almost unnoticed, Brack has crept up to third place in the points, only ten behind leader Stewart, 242, and a single point behind Scott Sharp. Sharp was a midfield 11th place finisher today. Foyt and Brack played the fuel card perfectly, as the winner coasted over the finish line, out of methanol, aided

by 11 laps under caution during his final run. Stewart, however, had to stop for a late splash of fuel, which took him out of contention for top honors. Stephan Gregoire and Davey Hamilton, both a lap down were fourth and fifth. Of note was the early and felicitous return to action of Billy Boat, just five weeks after he sustained a broken leg at New Hampshire. Although in pain, Boat retained his qualifying prowess, winning the pole and finishing ninth after running out of fuel two laps from the end. "The faster you go the better it feels," he noted.

Richard Dole

Pep Boys Indy Racing League Race 9
Atlanta 500 presented by MCI
Atlanta Motor Speedway
Hampton, GA
August 29, 1998
208 Laps, 320 Miles

KENNY BRACK MAKES IT THREE IN A ROW AT ATLANTA

Kenny Brack set an IRL record at Atlanta, three consecutive wins. He also set in motion a broad smile on the face of car owner A.J. Foyt, as

Brack assumed the lead in the points chase 282 to 259 over new second place man, Davey Hamilton, whom he replaced on the Foyt team. Hamilton was the runner-up today by .944 second. Previous points leader Tony Stewart started way back in 25th place, nursed a sub-normal engine into fifth place. He slipped to third place in the points race. Eddie Cheever notched his first podium since the Indianapolis 500, maintained that he was going "flat out" all day. Scott Goodyear secured another

"top five" with his fourth place. Billy Boat claimed his second pole in a row since returning from an injury mandated hiatus but failed to lead a lap. He lost a major encounter with Marco Greco that ended in the wall on lap 150, taking out Robby Unser and Steve Knapp as well. Jeff Ward, the second fastest qualifier, led the first 27 laps, was never thereafter a serious contender, finishing in sixth place. With only two races left, Brack is poised to give A.J. Foyt his first championship as a car owner.

Pep Boys Indy Racing League Race 10
Lone Star 500
Texas Motor Speedway
Fort Worth, TX
September 20, 1998
208 Laps, 312 Miles

JOHN PAUL JR. WINS AT TEXAS: HIS FIRST INDY CAR VICTORY SINCE 1983

John Paul Jr. has had a tough life as a racing driver. It started brilliantly with wins in the endurance racing team owned by his father and peaked with a thrilling last lap victory over Rick Mears in Championship Auto Racing Team's 500 mile race on the super fast Michigan Speedway in 1983. It went sharply downhill from there. The start of the new IRL was also the start of a new phase of his career. He had a strong run at Indianapolis this year which led to a full time ride with the Byrd-Cunningham Team. Their confidence in 38 year old Paul Jr. was rewarded with his victory at Texas under a broiling sun that may have led to multiple tire failures for the Goodyear runners. Paul Jr. avoided all the spins resulting from tire problems and driver error and had the horses to pass leader Jeff Ward with 16 laps to go. He built up a 1.577 second margin of victory at the checker. Team Cheever's young star Robby Unser also got past Ward to nail down runner-up honors. Roberto Guerrero finished fourth, an encouraging result for Infinity power. A conservative Kenny Brack drove at less than full tilt to avoid tire problems and protect his points lead with a fifth place finish. Paul Jr.'s win was a popular one on the circuit, where he is admired for his driving ability and low key approach. Tony Stewart's engine failure today made his quest for a repeat championship in the season finale appear to be an extremely difficult one but he and Davey Hamilton are still technically in contention for the title.

Pep Boys Indy Racing League Race 11
Las Vegas 500K
Las Vegas Motor Speedway
Las Vegas, NV
October 11, 1998
208 Laps, 312 Miles

ARIE LUYENDYK CLOSES OUT THE SEASON WITH VICTORY

THE TITLE AND $1 MILLION PEP BOYS BONUS GOES TO KENNY BRACK

Las Vegas fans hoping for a season-ending shootout between the three remaining title contenders, Kenny Brack, Davey Hamilton, and Tony Stewart were doomed to disappointment. None of the points leading trio were in contention. Brack had "black box" electrical problems, which, though eventually cured, put him six laps down in 11th at the checker. Hamilton crashed on lap 125, but was already three laps down when it happened. Stewart had undiagnosed engine problems right from the start but soldiered on to a 14th place finish. Denied the title shootout, the fans were treated to a winning performance by veteran Arie Luyendyk, who salvaged a subpar season with his convincing win in Las Vegas. He led the last 39 laps and had a .926 second cushion over fast closing Sam Schmidt at the checker. Buddy Lazier notched third place and John Paul Jr., who was a major factor all day, had two sessions in the lead, ended up fourth. "Steady Eddie" Cheever finished fifth. The final points standings were: Brack, 332, Hamilton, 292, Stewart, 289, Scott Sharp, 272, and Buddy Lazier, 262. Oldsmobile's Aurora engines powered every winner of the 11 race series.

U.S. Road Racing Championship

Richard Dole

King of the Can-Ams... Rob Dyson's stellar driving teams of Butch Leitzinger/James Weaver and Elliott Forbes-Robinson/Dorsey Schroeder won three of the five United States Road Racing Championship rounds in their well developed Riley & Scott Fords. Biggest disappointment was their failure to repeat their 1997 win, in the crown jewel of the series, the Rolex 24 at Daytona, which, like the season ending Watkins Glen 6 Hours fell to the Ferrari camp of Gianpiero Moretti. Weaver took the Driver's Championship over teammate Leitzinger by virtue of bonus points for pole position.

USRRC Race 1
Rolex 24 at Daytona
Daytona International Speedway
Daytona Beach, FL
January 31, 1998
24 Hours

**GIANPIERO MORETTI
AND HIS FERRARI FINALLY WIN
THE ROLEX 24 AT DAYTONA,
CROWN JEWEL OF THE
NEW U.S. ROAD
RACING CHAMPIONSHIP**

For more than a decade as car owner and driver Gianpiero Moretti had been trying, with unflagging enthusiasm and serious investment in equipment, to win the Rolex 24 at Daytona, his favorite race. His most recent entries, Ferrari 333SPs, had been on the pole and finished second, but never reached the charmed area of victory circle. In 1998, luck went his way and his all-star driving partners, Mauro Baldi, Arie Luyendyk, and Didier Theys, even let the 57 year old car owner drive the last 15 minutes to the checker. The car was eight laps

ahead when Moretti took in his final driving stint and kept it there. All the winning drivers receive Rolex watches but as, an ecstatic Moretti said, "For all the money I spent racing here, I could have bought a thousand Rolex watches." The luck that led to Moretti's win came in two phases; a failed gear on the pole winning Ferrari 333SP driven by Yannick Dalmas, Ron Fellows, Max Papis, and owner Andy Evans, which took a strong early lead. Phase two was the loss of power for the leading Dyson R&S Ford of Butch Leitzinger, James Weaver & Co. in the morning hours,

Daytona International Speedway

after 187 laps out front. A third bit of good fortune was overheating of the two Panoz GTR1 entries which were capable of putting severe pressure on the leaders, while Moretti's Ferrari trailed. Combined, these events were enough to give Moretti's car a huge lead. The next five finishers were all Porsches; a pair of GT1s driven by Uwe Alzen-Allan McNish, followed by Andre Aborle-Christophe Bouchut, taking first and second in GT1. Next up, Peter Kitchak-Franz Konrad, first in GT2 followed by John Graham-Duncan Halsmer, second in GT2. Even more surprising was the sixth

overall finish of the GT3 class winner, the BMW M3 of Bill Auberlen-Peter Cunningham followed by the GT3 runner-up, the Porsche driven by Mike Conte-Darryl Havens. Far back (75 laps behind the winner) was the second place Can-Am car (USRRC's name for World Sports Cars), Jim Downing's venerable Kudzu Mazda.

Once again, Daytona had proven that 24 hours can extract a toll on man and machine, but Moretti had borne repeated disappointment with good cheer and his win was a popular one. As the first and premier

event in the new U.S. Road Racing Championship, the Rolex 24 attracted more than 80 entries, 74 of which took the starter's flag.

The new series, sanctioned by the Sports Car Club of America, has scheduled four additional events Homestead, Mid-Ohio, Minneapolis, and Watkins Glen, competing with Professional Sports Car Racing, the sole group in international sports car racing in 1997. Like Daytona, Homestead and Watkins Glen are International Speedway Corporation venues.

USRRC Race 2
Homestead Motorsports Complex
Homestead, FL
May 17, 1998
2 Hours, 15 Minutes

DYSON DUO REBOUNDS TO TAKE HOMESTEAD VICTORY IN R&S FORD

Dyson Racing's star driving team of Butch Leitzinger and James Weaver had little success in their attempt to repeat their 1997 Rolex 24 at Daytona victory but bounced back in style to take the second round of the new USRRC Championship. Leitzinger was on the pole and the pair lost the lead only for two laps on a pit stop shuffle. Those two laps belonged to the Daytona winning Mauro Baldi-Gianpiero Moretti Ferrari 333SP, which outlasted the Dyson pair over the 24 Hour route but had to settle for second place here. At the two hour 15 minute Homestead length, the Dyson pair was never threatened, winning by 18.56 seconds. Only a single Panoz GTR1 contested this round. In the hands of Doc Bundy and Andy Wallace it was very much in the thick of things taking third overall and first in GT1.

A pair of GT3 entries, the BMWs of Ross Bentley-Marc Duez and Mark Simo-Boris Said beat all the GT2 cars, finishing seventh and eighth overall, first and second in class. GT2 class honors went to Terry Borchella-Scott Newman also in a BMW. An interesting feature of the race was a three pit stop requirement, which could have been a handicap for GT1 cars trying for the overall win on the basis of one less fuel stop. GT1 allows fuel tanks 3.3 gallons larger than the Can-Am class.

USRRC Race 3
Mid-Ohio Sports Car Complex
Lexington, OH
June 14, 1998
2 Hours, 30 Minutes

TWO IN A ROW FOR DYSON, ELLIOTT FORBES-ROBINSON AND DORSEY SCHROEDER WIN AT MID-OHIO

Panoz GTR1 driver David Brabham set the fastest race lap at Mid-Ohio, a heroic 103.82 mph, faster than James Weaver's pole-winning speed in Rob Dyson's R&S Ford Can-Am car. It was a gallant but failed effort to catch the two leading Dyson cars late in the race. Weaver's car had clutch problems which slowed him and co-driver Butch Leitzinger enough to let Dyson teammates Elliott Forbes-Robinson and Dorsey Schroeder pick up the victory, but not enough to keep them out of second place, overall and in the Can-Am class. Brabham and Andy Wallace finished third overall, on the same lap as the two Dyson cars, and first in GT1. Fourth overall, second in GT1, were the drivers of the second Panoz GTR1 Eric Bernard and Raul Boesel. Andy Pilgrim and Larry Schumacher copped the GT2 honors in a Porsche, but were upstaged by the BMW M3 of Bill Auberlen and Boris Said which finished one slot ahead of them, while taking first place in GT3. Winner Schroeder almost blew a huge lead in his last pit stop. He was given a "stop and wait" penalty for speeding in pit lane but still managed to beat the Leitzinger-Weaver team car by more than 15 seconds.

USRRC Race 4
Minneapolis Street Circuit
Minneapolis, MN
June 28, 1998
1 Hour, 45 Minutes

DYSON STEAMROLLER SWEEPS TO 1-2 VICTORY IN MINNEAPOLIS

There was no stopping Rob Dyson's two car entry of R&S Fords at Minneapolis. Pole-winning James Weaver with co-driver Butch Leitzinger led teammates Elliott Forbes-Robinson and Dorsey Schroeder to the checker by 22.057 seconds. Only one other car was on the same lap, the Panoz GTR1, driven by Doc Bundy and Johnny O'Connell, which claimed the top spot in GT1. Unlike some other occasions, the Panoz, a lone entry, was never a real threat to the two leaders. The Champion Porsche GT1, which finished fourth overall, second in GT1 might have made the GT1 race close, but an accident in qualifying forced drivers Thierry Boutsen and Bob Wollek to start 18th and last on a slippery track. The pair did carve their way through the field in exemplary fashion and even managed to lead for a few laps on a pit stop shuffle.

Once again, a GT3 car, the BMW M3 of Ross Bentley and Mark Simo beat all the GT2 runners, the best of which was another BMW driven by Peter Cunningham and Brian Simo. To date the Dyson forces have prevailed in three of the four USRRC events and appear headed for the championship with only a single event left on the calendar.

USRRC Race 5
First Union 6 Hours of the Glen
Watkins Glen International
Watkins Glen, NY
August 25, 1998
6 Hours

MORETTI FERRARI FLIES IN SEASON FINALE AT WATKINS GLEN

JAMES WEAVER TAKES THE CHAMPIONSHIP

It was the last race of the year for the new USRRC and the last race of his career for Ferrari 333SP owner/driver Gianpiero Moretti. Moretti left on a high note with a victory to match his season opening win in the Rolex 24 at Daytona. This time he didn't get to drive the final segment to the checker. That task befell co-driver Didier Theys, who had to fend off a hard charging James Weaver, in the Dyson R&S Ford, for the last quarter hour after a restart, a task he performed admirably. Weaver was a mere .656 second behind at the checker. Thierry Boutsen, in the Champion Porsche GT1, was very much involved in the upfront battle. With co-driver Ralf Kellener he led twice, finished third overall and first in GT1, the only other car to finish on the same lap as the leaders. The best Panoz finish was accomplished by the Eric Bernard-Raul Boesel coupe, which finished fourth overall, second in GT1. The other Panoz car collected the GT2 Porsche of Peter Argetsinger while attempting to lap it in the close company of Jon Field's R&S Ford. The GT2 and GT3 classes were a Porsche parade; again a GT3 car (Terry Borcheller-Randy Pobst) finished ahead of the first GT2 runner (Angelo Cilli-Trip Goolsby). In the course of the event, winner Theys managed to overcome a stop-and-go penalty for jumping a restart and third driver Mauro Baldi was a major factor in the Ferrari's success.

With the season ended, James Weaver became the USRRC's Can-Am Champion with 158 points to co-driver Butch Leitzinger's runner-up total of 154. Thierry Boutsen of the Champion Porsche team beat out Panoz's Eric Bernard for the GT1 crown, 147 to 120. In GT2, Mazda drivers Scott Sansone and Cameron Worth claimed the title with 140 points each despite the lack of any race wins. BMW's Ross Bentley was the GT3 titleist with 146 points over Porsche driver Danny Marshall with 101 points.

Denis L. Tanney

The Champion Porsche, winner in GT I, placed third overall, hounded the Can-Am leaders.

U.S. Road Racing Championship - Can-Am

U.S. Road Racing Championship's Can-Am Division was a **Rob Dyson** domaine. He's shown (center) with Champion **James Weaver**, (just left of Dyson) who scored 158 points. Third place **Elliott Forbes-Robinson** (just right of Dyson) had 144 points. Runner-up **Butch Leitzinger** (far left) had 154 points and fourth place **Dorsey Schroeder** (far right) earned 136 points.

Richard Dole

U.S. Road Racing Championship - Grand Touring

Champion Porsche's **Thierry Boutsen** (left) was the U.S. Road Racing Championship's GT1 Champion. He ran regularly with the leading Can-Am cars, earned 147 points.

Geoffrey Hewitt

BMW driver **Ross Bentley** (above) gained top honors in the U.S. Road Racing Championship's GT3 division with two victories and 146 points in the five race series.

Mazda RX-7 drivers **Scott Sansone** and **Cameron Worth** tied for the USRRC GT2 driver's title with 140 points despite the lack of a race win.

I have seen the enemy and the enemy is convention. The enemy is derivative. He is an endless repetition of apathy and mediocrity. And he better pray he never finds himself next to me at a stoplight

There is still one car on the road that refuses to conform. The V8 powered, 305 horse Panoz AIV Roadster. Hand-built by a car company that refuses to let the American roadster, and the ideas and beliefs that created it die. That company is Panoz Auto Development. For more information about our cars and our company visit us on the web at www.panozauto.com or call 1-888-GO-PANOZ (467-2660)

PROFESSIONAL SPORTS CAR RACING

Butch Leitzinger Lands the World Sports Car Championship... Again
Andy Wallace and David Brabham Share the Top GT Honors

This year in American endurance racing was different, very different. There were two separate series, each with its own sanctioning body. One thing remained the same. Butch Leitzinger of the Ford-powered Dyson Racing team took top honors in Professional Sports Car Racing's World Sports Car Championship for the second year in a row. He nailed down the title at 173 points, with second place in the season ending Laguna Seca round. Ferrari-mounted Wayne Taylor, winner of the first two WSC titles, was the runner-up with a 166 point total. The top two were season long rivals with the contest going down to the very end. Leitzinger won four of the season's eight events, added a second and two thirds, which translated to a podium appearance every time out. His team skipped two rounds, but he got a "guest" ride in one of these. Leitzinger practically grew up in endurance racing, entering his first Daytona 24 Hours in 1988 as a teenager. He shares the honor of the most WSC wins, 13, with teammate James Weaver and has captured eight poles and 24 victories in his 81 sports car endurance starts since then.

Runner-up Taylor, the driver who brought Oldsmobile a WSC manufacturer's title in the championship's first year and subsequently switched to Ferrari, won twice with Doyle-Risi teammate Eric van de Poele, who placed third in the championship with 155 points. The pair was the principal contributor to Ferrari's Manufacturer's

Championship, its third, including one tie. Leitzinger's teammate James Weaver, the series' wet weather star, took down fourth place in the title chase with 126. Dyson driver Dorsey Schroeder, a former top competitor in the Trans-Am ranks, collected 110 points for fifth place at season's end. Jon Field was named Most Improved Driver.

In the top GT ranks, GT1, if you weren't driving a Panoz GTR1, you weren't in the top four. Panoz Racing's Andy Wallace and David Brabham shared championship honors with 176 points. Third place went to teammates Eric Bernard (169) and Raul Boesel (84). Porsche driver Thierry Boutsen of the Champion Racing team at 76 points, completed the top five. Panoz ran away with the Manufacturer's Championship over Porsche 197 to 97 and the Team Championship by an even wider margin. Shane Lewis got Most Improved Driver honors. On more than one occasion the fleet, front engined Panoz coupes came within an eyelash of the overall win in close contests with the highly ranked and faster qualifying WSC cars. At the fall Sebring race they made it stick. Brabham and Wallace took the overall win.

At the season ending Laguna Seca round only a banzai finish by Bill Auberlen in a factory backed BMW 8 cylinder spyder nipped the leading Panoz coupe at the finish, after Andy Wallace put it on the pole.

In GT2, Porsche driver Larry Schumacher, the Mosports winner,

prevailed in the title quest with 148 points over runner-up teammate John O'Steen with 106. A third Porsche driver Franz Konrad, the Sebring and Laguna Seca winner, placed third with 76 points. Marc Duez scored three wins but no other points for fourth place. BMW's Andy Pilgrim won at Las Vegas on his way to 67 points and fifth place in GT2. David Friedman was the division's Most Improved Driver. Porsche captured the Manufacturer's Championship and team honors went to Schumacher Racing.

GT3 was all BMW. Prototype Technology's Mark Simo edged teammate and 1997 champion Bill Auberlen for the title with 177 points to 175. Another BMW pair, Peter Cunningham and Ross Bentley, clocked in with 164 and 148 points for the third and fourth slots. Porsche driver Cort Wagner salvaged fifth place with 148 points and a fine win at Laguna Seca. Not surprisingly, the Manufacturer's Championship went to BMW and the team title was awarded to Prototype Technology. Darryl Havens was named GT3's Most Improved Driver.

The season's big developments were Ford-powered Leitzinger's repeat Driver's Championship, the ability of the Panoz GT coupes to compete with WSC cars for the overall win, and the successful Road Atlanta preview of next year's American Le Mans Series, which accepts (and encourages) factory prototypes. The American Le Mans Series also announced network TV coverage.

SPORTS CAR RACING'S RENAISSANCE MAN

Donald Panoz is applying the same energy and business acumen that gained him a pharmaceutical fortune to a new business, sports car racing. In a few short years he has accumulated, using his own money, an amazing number of enterprises in what shapes up to be a full fledged motorsports conglomerate. Among them Panoz Motor Developments, producer of the swift but spartan AIV roadster, Panoz Motorsports, the Visteon sponsored racing team which produces and campaigns its own highly successful Ford powered cars, the Panoz GTR1, three prime road courses, Road Atlanta, Sebring, and Mosport, the new for 1999 American Le Mans Series, patterned after France's famed 24 hour event, an all-girl racing series, logically titled the Women's Global GT Series. A series for the legendary drivers of the recent past under the Super Stars of Auto Racing banner is on the drawing board. There's even a new driving school in conjunction with Subaru on top of the separate Panoz Driving School.

In the course of upgrading Road Atlanta to the level where it could be a serious contender for a Formula One race it also became an even more serious contender for a FedEx Champ Car race, possibly as early as 2000. Nearby, Panoz built the magnificent 3300 acre Chateau Elan Winery and Resort with all the luxurious guest facilities of Europe's best - and its own PGA Tour tournament. A winery in Georgia? If anyone can make it work Don Panoz can. He might even be able to provide the catalyst to combine U.S. sports car racing's two rival sanctioning groups, the USRRC and Professional SportsCar Racing, which went their own separate ways in 1998 and plan to do the same in 1999. Panoz has opted for PSCR to sanction his American Le Mans Series. He is converting at least one of his GTR1 coupes to an open World Sports Car which would make it eligible for the USRRC, which does not accept GT1 hardtops, as well as the American Le Mans Series. Panoz is at home with major undertakings. His latest: Diablo Grande, a 42 square mile golf/residential community in California's San Joaquin Valley. The plans call for 12,000 residents, 50 acres of vineyards, a resort hotel and spa. Two world class golf courses are already operational.

If all this sounds like a lot for one man to take on, consider that, starting at age 25, without family wealth, he founded two major pharmaceutical companies, Mylan laboratories and Elan Corporation. Along the way he was awarded two dozen patents, including the one for the nicotine patch.

Richard Dole

HARDCHARGING HARDTOPS
Panoz's GTR1s easily won PSCR's competitive GT1 drivers, manufacturers, and team championships, on occasion threatened the World Sports Car front runners for the overall win.

Donald Panoz

PANOZ MOTORSPORTS INITIATIVES

GT RACERS: Panoz GTR1s captured the GT1 Drivers, Manufacturers, and Team Championships in the Professional SportsCar Racing series, on occasions pressured the higher rated World Sports Cars for the overall win. The cars are unique front engine coupes powered by pushrod Ford engines, similar to NASCAR powerplants.

RACE SERIES: Panoz's new for 1999 American Le Mans Series licenses the name and adopts the rules of France's famed 24 Hour endurance event. Sanctioned by Professional SportsCar Racing, the series' first event, at Sebring in March, is expecting such exotic entries as the Audi R8 and the BMW V12 LMR, as well as Ferrari 333SPs, and Riley & Scott Fords. Eight races scheduled, all with network TV coverage.

RACE CIRCUITS: Redesigned, refurbished and polished to a fine gloss, Panoz's Road Atlanta was a serious candidate for the Formula One event that went to Indianapolis in 2000. It is now an even more serious candidate for a CART FedEx Championship race in 2000. It will host the second round of Panoz's new American Le Mans series. Sebring and Mosport, the other two Panoz circuits will also host ALMS races.

Richard Dole

ROAD CARS: The Panoz Roadster AIV, now in its third year of production, is a "purist's car." Retro styling, a high performance aluminum engine (Ford's 305 horsepower DOHC 4.6), space age materials, including an aluminum chassis, give the AIV outstanding performance. Air conditioning and a 180 watt stereo are standard but other frills are lacking. The 2000 model Esperante incorporates more mainstream exotic car styling and comforts but employs the same high tech, low maintenance approach of the roadster.

RACING SCHOOLS: Subaru-Panoz Performance Driving School focuses on braking, steering, skid control, and defensive driving tactics. It employs a fleet of 1999 Legacy 2.5 GTs, headquartered at Road Atlanta. It's separate from the Panoz Driving School which concentrates on high performance, racing oriented skills using Panoz coupes as school cars.

WOMEN'S GLOBAL GT SERIES, under its Indy 500 veteran executive director Lyn St. James, attracted 80 candidates for tryouts. Forty-two were cleared to drive in the series' Esperante WGGTSs. Among the fastest, Portland's Cindy Lynx and England's Divina Galica. A six race schedule will support ALMS events. With St. James, right, at the tryouts are Nancy and Don Panoz.

RESORTS: Close to Road Atlanta, Chateau Elan Winery and Resort is a magnificent 3300 acre installation with luxurious guest facilities matching Europe's best. It boasts a year round schedule of wine and sports-related events highlighted by November's Sarazen World Open, a stop on the PGA Tour.

After 351 laps at the most grueling 24-hour endurance race in the world, we have only one thing to say. Cheese! Not only did we take 1st and 2nd, but we did it in both the Le Mans GT1 and GT2. And if that's not enough to get our snapshot taken, there's always our victories at the FIA GT2 Championship and Sebring. To find out how Pilot® tires can make you smile a whole lot wider, call 1.888.MICHELIN or visit us at michelin.com/pilot.

Because so much is riding on your tires.

First and second at **Le Mans.** So when do we get our picture on the cereal box?

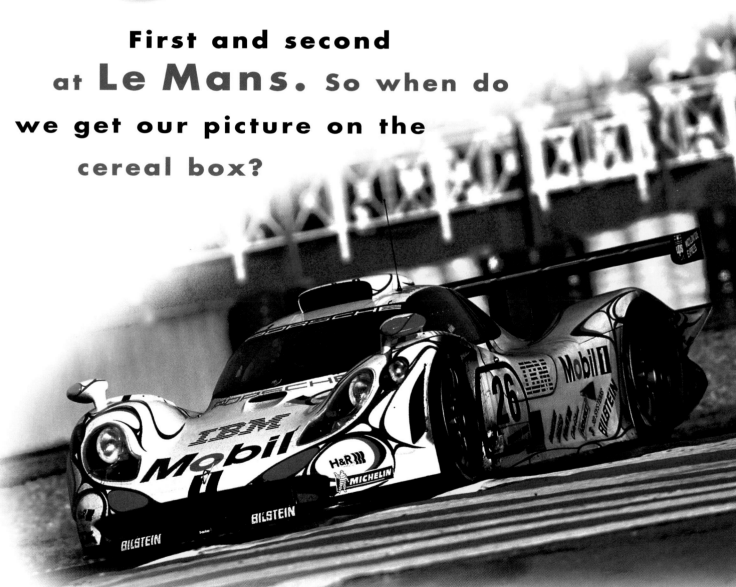

Professional Sports Car Race 1
Exxon Superflo 12 Hours of Sebring
Sebring International Raceway
Sebring, FL
March 21, 1998
12 Hours

MOMO FERRARI PREVAILS OVER A PAIR OF PURSUING PANOZ GT COUPES AT SEBRING

Sebring, the oldest continuous endurance race in the U.S., is steeped in legend and always attracts a substantial entry. 1998 was no exception, with 48 cars taking the starter's flag for the long haul ahead. First off was the Toshiba Ferrari 333SP that Wayne Taylor put on the pole at the newly reconfigured course with a 115.773 mph lap. Four laps into the race, the Carolina Turkey R&S Ford, listing a veteran driving team of David Murry, Hurley Haywood, and Derek Bell, who cer-

tainly owned, collectively, more endurance victories than any other team in the contest, took over. Next to gain the lead, on lap 12, was the MOMO Ferrari 333SP with an all-star international driver lineup of Didier Theys, Gianpiero Moretti, and Mauro Baldi. This would be the first of nine sessions in the lead for this strong campaigner. Their last and decisive move was on lap 258 when the Ferrari team displaced the strong Andy Wallace-David Brabham Panoz Ford GTR1 from its four lap run out front. The Ferrari then ran out the clock, completing 319 laps. The gallant Panoz pair finished second, just over a lap down at 318, followed by the Champion Porsche 911 GT1 handled by Thierry Boutsen, Bob Wollek, and Andy Pilgrim, also with 318 laps completed. The second Panoz, driven by Eric Bernard, Jamie Davies, and Doc Bundy, crossed the line in fourth place with 312 laps. Fifth overall went to the surprising GT2 Porsche 911 turbo of Nick Ham.

The second best WSC car, the pole-sitting Taylor-van de Poele-Fermin Velez Ferrari 333SP, salvaged sixth place overall after having been a strong contender in the first quarter of the long event. Second in GT2 went to the Saleen Mustang of Steve Saleen, Ron Johnson, and Tommy Archer, in seventh place overall at 297 laps. A pair of BMW M3s nabbed GT3 honors; Bill Auberlen and Boris Said recording 295 laps and Peter Cunningham-Ross Bentley-Mark Simo checking in with 293. The third place in the WSC category went to the Safety Glow R&S Ford of Dorsey Schroeder, Butch Leitzinger, and James Weaver, one of the pre-race favorites, with 290 laps and 13th place overall. Third place in GT3 was claimed by the Cort Wagner-Darryl Havens Porsche 911 RSR with 286 laps.

With the exception of the MOMO Ferrari, it was a day in which the GTs soundly outran the favored WSC entries.

Professional Sports Car Race 2
Toshiba Nevada Grand Prix
Las Vegas Motor Speedway
Las Vegas, NV
April 26, 1998
3 Hours, 45 Minutes

FERRARI EDGES PANOZ AT LAS VEGAS

A mere .445 second separated Wayne Taylor's winning Ferrari 333SP from David Brabham's Panoz GTR1 at the end of Las Vegas' exciting three hour and 45 minute race. This pair, along with co-drivers Eric van de Poele in the Ferrari and Andy Wallace in the Panoz exchanged the lead seven times in the course of the event, with Brabham setting the fastest race lap. The only other car in contention was the R&S Ford of Jim Matthews and David Murry, which led twice before being sidelined with a broken oil line. The third place finisher was Jim Downing's Kudzu Mazda, a hefty 13 laps behind the pair fighting for the lead up front, but good for WSC runner-up honors. Next in line at the finish was a trio of BMWs from Prototype Technology which checked in first in GT2 (Bill Auberlen-Boris Said), first in GT3 (Marc Duez-Mark Simo), and second in GT3 (Ross Bentley-Peter Cunningham). Porsche-mounted Larry Schumacher claimed second place in a three car GT2 field, with Bill Eagles in a Vector, the third man in the group. Although the starting field was slim, the faithful spectators were treated to a close contest and some great racing by virtue of the Taylor-Brabham battle.

Dan Bianchi

Professional Sports Car Race 3
Dodge Dealers Grand Prix
Lime Rock Park
Lakeville, CT
May 25, 1998
1 Hour, 45 Minutes

DYSON R&S FORD HOME FIRST AT LIME ROCK. GT RACE GOES TO PANOZ

A win is a win even if it's over only eight competitors. Rob Dyson's R&S Ford, with star drivers Butch Leitzinger and James Weaver at the helm, was clearly the best of the nine WSC entries. It was the first Dyson win at Lime Rock, the team's "home territory," despite multiple victories elsewhere. At Lime Rock the WSC and GT cars had separate one and three-quarter hour events, so there were no troublesome Panoz GTs to contest top honors as there had been at Las Vegas. Leitzinger was on the pole and ran off the first 41 laps out front before giving way to perennial rival, Wayne Taylor in the Toshiba Ferrari, for 28 laps. Fredy Lienhard's Lista Ferrari then had eight laps in the lead before surrendering the top spot to the Dyson Ford with Weaver cruising to an 18.375 second margin at the finish.

In the separate GT event, the year's dominating Panoz team scored a one-two, with the Andy Wallace-David Brabham duo two laps ahead of teammate Eric Bernard and Raul Boesel at the finish. Shane Lewis and Vic Rice got their sometimes quirky Rapter going for third overall, third in GT1. GT2 and GT3 again belonged to the BMW forces; Marc Duez and Boris Said were atop GT2, while Ross Bentley and Peter Cunningham took GT3 honors. The Larry Schumacher-Joe Varde Porsche finished second in GT2 with another Porsche driven by David Friedman, while Todd Snyder was third. Cort Wagner and Darryl Havens collected the third podium position in GT3. The two Panoz cars exchanged the lead three times but nobody else came close.

Professional Sports Car Race 4
Road Atlanta
Braselton, GA
June 21, 1998
3 Hours, 45 Minutes

DYSON R&S FORDS FINISH FIRST AND SECOND AT ROAD ATLANTA

Butch Leitzinger and James Weaver were the class of the field at Road Atlanta. Their toughest opposition came from Dyson Racing teammates Dorsey Schroeder and Elliott Forbes-Robinson in the team's second R&S Ford, and even this pair

was 44.891 seconds in arrears at the end. Eric van de Poele was the fastest qualifier in the Toshiba Ferrari 333SP but he fell to Leitzinger after 14 laps in front. The remarkable Champion Porsche 911 GT1 of Thierry Boutsen and Bob Wollek then took over the top spot for seven laps. The rest was all Dyson with the Leitzinger-Weaver car running off the last 120 laps in the lead unchallenged. Boutsen and Wollek mounted a gallant effort, good for first in GT, but were no match for the Dyson WSC cars. Van de Poele and Wayne Taylor salvaged fourth place overall, third in WSC. The Panoz team, which had been harassing the lead WSC

cars in recent events was non-threatening today despite entering three cars on their hometrack. The best of the lot was the Raul Boesel-Eric Bernard pairing, 18 laps off the pace but still good for second place in GT1. Teammates Doc Bundy and Johnny O'Connell lost their transmission while Andy Wallace was involved in an accident.

In GT2 it was BMW again with Marc Duez and Brian Simo ahead of the Larry Schumacher-John O'Steen Porsche.

GT3 again fell to BMW with Bill Auberlen and Mark Simo edging out teammates Peter Cunningham and Ross Bentley.

Professional Sports Car Race 5
Mosport International Raceway
Bowmansville, Canada
August 9, 1998
2 Hours, 45 Minutes

DYSON R&S FORDS MASTER MOSPORT

For the second race in a row Rob Dyson's R&S Fords finished first and second, with the Butch Leitzinger-James Weaver pair showing the way to teammates Elliott Forbes-Robinson and Dorsey Schroeder. Team owner Rob Dyson

is determined to wrest the lead in the Driver's Championship from Ferrari driver Wayne Taylor and appears to be on the verge of doing just that. Taylor and Eric van de Poele finished sixth overall, fourth in WSC. After the race the points stood Taylor, 110, van de Poele, 109, Leitzinger, 106, with three races to go. The Panoz forces, after a bad day at hometrack Atlanta, rebounded for third (David Brabham-Andy Wallace) and fourth (Eric Bernard-Raul Boesel) overall; first and second in GT1. Each led a few laps, both were a lap down at the finish. Fifth overall, third in WSC, was

the Lista Ferrari of Didier Theys and Fredy Lienhard. The BMWs had a field day. Bill Auberlen and Mark Simo scored first in GT3 ahead of GT3 teammates Ross Bentley and Peter Cunningham, both beating the team's GT2 winning car driven by Marc Duez and Ross Bentley. Larry Schumacher and John O'Steen, in a Porsche, placed second in GT2. Third place in GT2 went to John Morton and John Graham in a Porsche. Another Porsche, driven by Cort Wagner and Darryl Havens scored third in GT3. Fifteen cars took the starter's flag.

Professional Sports Car Race 6
NAPA Sebring Classic
Sebring International Raceway
Sebring, FL
September 19, 1998
3 Hours

ANDY WALLACE & DAVID BRABHAM GIVE PANOZ ITS FIRST OVERALL VICTORY AT RAINY SEBRING

Certainly the narrower Michelin tires helped on a rain plagued Sebring track, so waterlogged, the race was red flagged at one point, but drivers Andy Wallace and David Brabham get full marks for bringing their Panoz GTR1 home first overall in the treacherous conditions. They'd been close to an outright win before

and this time the elements gave them the little edge they needed. The elements were less kind to Ferrari driver Wayne Taylor, who was leading the points race prior to this event. He crashed into the wall and out of action on a mid-race restart. The mishap allowed Butch Leitzinger, second overall today and first in WSC, with co-driver James Weaver, to take over the points lead 132 to 122. The other Dyson R&S Ford with Dorsey Schroeder and Elliott Forbes-Robinson claimed third overall, second in WSC. Weather was the key, as the race unfolded. First, eight minutes of dry running with polesitter Taylor setting the pace, then an hour and a half of yellow flag plus red flag conditions. The green came out for

less than a minute, the period in which Taylor hit the wall followed by another 65 minutes under yellow. During the last 16 minutes a soggy green flag waved. In this period Wallace nabbed the lead for four laps and victory. The winners' average speed speaks for the conditions, 40.582 mph. An R&S Ford driven by Henry Camferdam and Scott Shubot was fourth overall, third in WSC.

GT2 honors went to the Porsche pair of Larry Schumacher and John O'Steen.

Cort Wagner and Kelly Collins collected GT3 honors in a Porsche RSR. When things finally dried out, the day's big item was the Panoz overall win, a major accomplishment under any conditions.

Professional Sports Car Race 7
Petit Le Mans
Road Atlanta Motorsports Complex
Braselton, GA
October 10, 1998
391 Laps, 1000 Miles

WAYNE TAYLOR AND FERRARI REBOUND TO CAPTURE THE INAUGURAL PETIT LE MANS

Don Panoz's American Le Mans Series, slated to start in 1999, passed its first hurdle in Road Atlanta's Petit Le Mans, a 1000 mile endurance grind, designed to test the new format. It attracted two Porsche factory entries, one in the Le Mans Prototype class that was lumped with WSC in the scoring. Porsche's GT car, designated GT1-98, driven by Yannick Dalmas and Alan McNish, dominated the first half of the race. It was leading by two laps when it got too close to the other factory entry, the Porsche LMP1-98, lost downforce and performed a spectacular back flip before landing on its tail. Unbelievably, the driver, Dalmas, was unhurt. The car wasn't so lucky. This mishap handed the lead to the Panoz GTR1 driven by David Brabham and Andy Wallace, which swapped the lead with Taylor's Ferrari before falling out with oiling problems. With the Panoz out of contention, Taylor's Ferrari was too strong for the Porsche LMP1-98 which finished on the same lap. The third finisher, the Champion Porsche GT1 Evo driven by Thierry Boutsen and Bob Wollek, claimed the top spot in GT1. With his regular Dyson Ford not entered, Butch Leitzinger was fortunate to get a ride with the Support Net R&S Ford that finished fourth overall. His lead over Taylor in the championship chase was reduced to four, 151 to 147. The Dyson entry will be back for the season finale so the championship battle will go down to the wire. GT2 honors went to Porsche-mounted Michel Ligonett and Lance Stewart. GT3 winners were Porsche drivers Peter Argetsinger and Angelo Cilli, who bested the BMWs today.

Richard Dole

BMW GRABS THE VICTORY IN WORLD SPORTS CAR DEBUT AT LAGUNA SECA. BUTCH LEITZINGER TAKES HIS SECOND TITLE.

American Bill Auberlen was the hero of BMW's successful debut in World Sports Car competition with a stirring late race charge to the checker. Taking over from co-driver Didier Rodrigues, he went from a half minute deficit to the leading Panoz coupes to a 5.722 second margin of victory at the checker. With the race starting under rainy conditions, the Panoz GTR1 coupes with their Michelin rain tires, narrower than those on the WSC entries, had an advantage and alternated the lead for the first 43 laps. Andy Wallace had already demonstrated the Ford-powered coupe's potential; by qualifying on the pole in the dry, beating all the WSC contingent. Although Butch Leitzinger got his R&S Ford out in front for nine laps, he was destined to finish fourth (with co-driver James Weaver) two places ahead of arch rival Wayne Taylor in a Ferrari 333SP. The fourth place gave him his second WSC Driver's Championship in a row. The front running Panoz coupes claimed the runner-up (Wallace and David Brabham) and third place honors overall (Eric Bernard and Johnny O'Connell), as well as first and second in GT1.

Fifth overall and tops in GT2 was the surprising Porsche of Franz Konrad and Jan Lammers. Cort Wagner and David Murry drove the Porsche which claimed tenth overall and first in GT3.

The day's major items were the successful BMW debut, Leitzinger's retention of his title, and another strong battle for the overall win by the Panoz GT teams. The team gained the GT Driver's Championship, a tie between Wallace and Brabham, the Manufacturer's Championship, and the team title. Larry Schumacher upheld Porsche honor with his GT2 title and BMW's Mark Simo corraled the year's GT3 driver's honors.

Professional Sports Car Racing - World Sports Car

1 Repeat Champion... **Butch Leitzinger** needed a "guest ride" at Road Atlanta to keep his title since his team missed two events, but prevail he did. (173 PSCR points)

2 Two Time Champion... **Wayne Taylor** just missed a third title. (166 PSCR points)

3 Taylor Teammate... **Eric van de Poele**, helped his team to two victories. (156 PSCR points)

4 Leitzinger Teammate... **James Weaver** was a big contributor to his team's four wins. (126 PSCR points)

Richard Dole

Richard Dole

Professional Sports Car Racing - Grand Touring

Panoz Parade... The first four slots in GT1 went to Panoz drivers. **David Brabham** and **Andy Wallace** (right) tied for the Driver's Championship with 176 points each. **Eric Bernard** (left) captured third place with 169, and **Raul Boesel** (far left) was fourth with 84.

Photos: Richard Dole

Porsche Protagonist...
Larry Schumacher repeated his GT2 title. (148 points)

BMW Buddies... This time **Mark Simo** (left), with 177 points, got the nod over **Bill Auberlen** (right), with 175 points, for the Driver's Championship in GT3.

BARBER DODGE PRO SERIES

ROOKIE JEFF SIMMONS TAKES THE TITLE AND $300,000 BONUS
19 New Track Records Set in First Year with Michelin-Shod Reynard Chassis

The reliable 250 hp Dodge V6s were the same, the chassis, carbon fiber Reynards fitted with 6-speed sequential gearboxes, and Michelin Pilot tires were all new. The result; 19 new track records, including seven record qualifying speeds in the 12 race series for equally prepared "spec" single-seaters. The series set new marks off the track as well. Champion Jeff Simmons' "Career Enhancement" bonus set a new mark at $300,000 as did his total prize money of $378,500. Rookie Simmons earned his title. Starting in only 11 of the 12 events, he won three times, each time leading every lap from a record setting pole position. His road to the top of the charts was hotly contested and not decided until the final Laguna Seca round. Simmons' season long adversary, Todd Snyder, who had won twice previously and scored a single pole, came up with an all-out effort, leading every lap in a clear cut victory. Simmons, however, was not to be denied the title. His runner-up 16 points earned him the championship by a three point margin for the year, 158 to 155, over Snyder. The Barber Dodge rules allow only a driver's best ten results to be counted.

Snyder's prize money for the year was $77,300 only $1,200 less than champion Simmons - without the big bonus. The two top points earners were Americans in a multi-national driver line-up of developing talent.

Norway's Thomas Schie was third on the year's honor list with 114 points. He won twice and garnered a single pole, but was never a threat to the two leaders down the stretch, suffering two early exits in the last four events. Giovanni Anapoli of Italy was runner-up at Road America, his best effort, but his consistency gained him fourth place for the year at 103 points. Will Langhorne led every lap of his Grand Rapids win but three disappointing outings left him in fifth place with 98 points. Brazil's Nilton Rossoni showed a high turn of speed, documented by his pair of victories, pair of poles. Unfortunately, he missed four events and even his win and third place in the last two races couldn't get him into the top five. Sixth place at 83 points was the lot for this talented pilot. Seventh place went to another Brazilian, Nicolas Rondet, who missed three races and scored 67 points, but no wins or poles. Californian Jon Fogarty was the come-from-behind winner on the

challenging Mid-Ohio circuit. A third place was the best of his other efforts. He scored 65 points, good for eighth place. The Netherlands' Sepp Foster was on the pole for the opening Sebring round, led the first lap, exited shortly thereafter. He had almost equally poor luck as the season developed but still made the top ten with 61 points. Last driver to earn a top ten ranking was Alex Gurney, son of racing legend Dan Gurney. His standout event was the penultimate round at Homestead where he claimed the pole and finished fourth. We'll be hearing more from him.

Among the records set for the year were $1.1 million in prize money and the 2.753 million households viewing Barber Dodge on TV.

Of note among the Barber Dodge Pro Series alumni, 1996 Champion Kenny Brack was the 1998 Pep Boys Indy Racing League Champion, and 1991 Champion Bryan Herta won his first FedEx Championship Series race. Brack was the only other Barber Dodge Champion, prior to Simmons, to win as a rookie. The Barber Dodge Pro Series seems to be meeting its goal of getting graduates into the PPG-Dayton Indy Lights Series and on to the top level of IRL and CART.

Barber Dodge Pro Series Race 1
Sebring Road Course
Sebring, FL
March 21, 1998
17 Laps, 41:54 Minutes

TODD SNYDER CLAIMS THE VICTORY IN SEBRING'S SEASON OPENER

The Netherlands' Sepp Koster was the surprise polesitter in the first race of the year, the first with the new equipment package of Reynard chassis, Michelin Pilot tires, powered by the same Dodge single cam V6 engines. Koster seemingly mastered the new car more quickly than his peers and set a new record, 101.724 mph in qualifying on the pole. After leading the first lap his race was over. The next 16 laps and the victory belonged to Todd Snyder who set a record race lap at 101.442 mph and a record race average speed (90.083 mph) along the way. Runner-up Victor Gonzalez Jr. was 5.325 seconds in arrears at the checker. Norway's Thomas Schie was a solid third.

Barber Dodge Pro Series Race 2
Lime Rock Park
Lakeville, CT
May 25, 1998
30 Laps, 33:54 Minutes

THOMAS SCHIE SCORES AT LIME ROCK, HOME BASE FOR BARBER DODGE

Norway's Thomas Schie, whose closing surge fell short in the Sebring season opener made it stick this time. He took over the lead from Rino Mastronardi with six laps to go and was still leading when the race ended under caution. A charging Todd Snyder, who also got by Mastronardi, was denied the opportunity of a late race shootout by the yellow flag. He settled for second place but surely would have been a factor had the race stayed green. Mastronardi finished third. Rookie Jeff Simmons, in his first start of the year, turned the fastest race lap at 100.895 mph. Polesitter Nicolas Rondet was in command for the first 13 laps before handing over the lead to Mastronardi. He placed fourth.

Barber Dodge Pro Series Race 3
The Circuit at Belle Isle Park
Detroit, MI
June 7, 1998
20 Laps, 40:12 Minutes

ROOKIE JEFF SIMMONS DOMINATES IN DETROIT, WINS FROM THE POLE

In his second outing with the new Reynard-Dodge-Michelin package rookie Jeff Simmons clearly had mastered its nuances. He was on the pole at 91.899 mph, led every lap including the race's fastest at a record 92.065 mph. Will Langhorne, recovering from a disappointing outing in the season opener, was a competitive runner-up, .820 second behind at the checker. Rino Mastronardi checked in with his second third place finish in a row. Sepp Koster, the Sebring polesitter, was fourth, while young Rocky Moran Jr., son of the Indy car driver, completed the top five. Todd Snyder, the Sebring winner and runner-up at Lime Rock, could do no better than sixth today.

Skip Barber Racing

Richard Dole

Barber Dodge Pro Series Race 4
Watkins Glen Short Course
Watkins Glen, NY
June 28, 1998
24 Laps, 41:05 Minutes

Barber Dodge Pro Series Race 5
Burke Lakefront Airport
Cleveland, OH
July 12, 1998
25 Laps, 41:07 Minutes

Barber Dodge Pro Series Race 6
Grand Rapids Street Course
Grand Rapids, MI
July 26, 1998
30 Laps, 40:27 Minutes

JEFF SIMMONS MAKES IT TWO IN A ROW AT WATKINS GLEN

Jeff Simmons is setting a torrid pace in his campaign for the Barber Dodge title and the $300,000 year end bonus. Watkins Glen's short course became the second circuit in a row to fall to his skills. He again led every one of the race's 24 laps from the pole. Despite never being out of the lead, Simmons had plenty of opposition. Runner-up Nilton Rossoni was only .510 second behind at the checker after setting the fastest race lap at 116.359 mph. Rocky Moran Jr. captured third place, his best effort of the year. Todd Snyder posted his poorest performance of the season, just making the race's top ten. Samer Hindi, in fourth place at the finish, had his best outing of the year. Sepp Koster rounded out the top five. Tom Schie finished sixth today.

THOMAS SCHIE SCORES ON CLEVELAND'S WIDE STRAIGHTS

Cleveland's wide straights and generous run-off areas make for some interesting and widely varied cornering lines. Thomas Schie found them suited to his driving style. He ran down polesitter Nilton Rossoni of Brazil, who led the first 19 laps and ran away to a 1.300 second margin at the finish. When Rossoni went out of contention, runner-up honors went to another Brazilian Nicolas Rondet. A fast closing Jeff Simmons took down third place, just ahead of rival Todd Snyder who garnered the race's fastest lap at 100.042 mph. Canada's John McCaig completed the top five list. With Schie becoming the season's second two time winner the championship is truly developing as a three way battle among Simmons, Snyder, and Schie.

WILL LANGHORNE GAINS THE GRAND RAPIDS VICTORY

No he wasn't on the pole; Victor Gonzalez Jr. was, but Virginian Will Langhorne led every lap of the Grand Rapids street race. Gonzalez didn't even make the top five. Langhorne's margin of victory was 2.910 seconds over Jeff Simmons who aided his own championship campaign with the 16 points that go to the runner-up. Simmons also came in with the fastest race lap on lap 15 at 75.483 mph. Title rival Todd Snyder checked in in seventh place, while Cleveland winner Thomas Schie was out of the points in 19th place. Nicolas Rondet garnered third place. The fourth spot went to Giovanni Anapoli of Italy, his best result of the year. The polesitter in Cleveland, Nilton Rossoni, completed the top five line-up.

Barber Dodge Pro Series Race 7	Barber Dodge Pro Series Race 8	Barber Dodge Pro Series Race 9
Mid-Ohio Road Course	Road America	Laguna Seca Raceway
Lexington, OH	Elkhart Lake, Wi	Monterey, CA
August 9, 1998	August 16, 1998	September 13, 1998
25 Laps, 40:11 Minutes	17 Laps, 40:57 Minutes	25 Laps, 42:20 Minutes

JON FOGARTY FLIES IN SURPRISE MID-OHIO VICTORY

Four lead changes made the Mid-Ohio round the most competitive of the seven Barber Dodge Pro Series events to date. The last change, on lap 18, elevated Jon Fogarty into the top spot, which he held to the end, building up a comfortable margin of 16.513 seconds. That pass came at the expense of Todd Snyder who ended up fourth. Fourth was substantially better than the fate that befell arch rival Jeff Simmons; he dropped out after taking the lead from Giovanni Anapoli on lap five and was scored 26th and last. Anapoli had a happier outing; he was third at the checker. Thomas Schie was the polesitter. He was in front only for the first lap, finished eighth. Fifth place at the end went to Alex Gurney, his best outing of the year. Fogarty had made the top ten only once previously.

NILTON ROSSONI ROLLS AT ROAD AMERICA

The last time Nilton Rossoni was on the pole, at Cleveland, he had nothing but a 21st place finish to show for his qualifying speed. This time was different. The Brazilian set a new record in qualifying, 108.813 mph and led every lap from the pole position. He was a comfortable 3.932 seconds ahead of runner-up Giovanni Anapoli at the finish and posted a record 109.277 mph race lap along the way. Anapoli is becoming one of the more consistent drivers on the circuit. Todd Snyder's third place gained him three points on rival Jeff Simmons who placed fifth today. Fourth went to the other Brazilian, Nicolas Rondet. Thomas Schie, noted for his qualifying prowess, was only 14th fastest this time but moved up to sixth place at the end, earning him the race's "Progressive Driver" award.

TODD SNYDER SCORES AT LAGUNA SECA

Todd Snyder set another record in qualifying, 93.697 mph, and followed it up with a wire-to-wire victory run. Right on his tailpipes was arch rival Jeff Simmons, a slim .431 second behind at the end. Jon Fogarty, demonstrating that his Mid-ohio win was no fluke, finished third. Young Rocky Moran Jr. set a new record race lap of 92.760 mph, finished fourth. Unfortunately, it appears unlikely that he'll be able to make the next two rounds. Road America winner Nicolas Rossoni and his compatriot Nicolas Rondet both were non-starters here. Thomas Schie, a title contender earlier, was scored in 23rd place, lost considerable ground to the leaders. Snyder and Simmons appear capable of carrying their title fight down to the final round - again at Laguna Seca. Look for a renewal of this crowd pleasing rivalry.

Richard Dole

BARBER DODGE PRO SERIES

Champion Jeff Simmons reaps one of his rewards, a $300,000 "Career Enhancement" bonus presented by Barber Dodge founding father Skip Barber.

Simmons' Michelin-shod, Dodge-powered Reynard set three new records at Road Atlanta, qualifying (109.437 mph), race average speed (102.240 mph), and fastest race lap (109.342 mph). Atlanta was one of three races he won from the pole.

Richard Dole

Barber Dodge Pro Series Race 10
Road Atlanta
Braselton, GA
October 10, 1998
27 Laps, 40:33 Minutes

JEFF SIMMONS ROLLS AT ROAD ATLANTA

At Road Atlanta's beautifully refinished road course, Jeff Simmons turned the table on arch rival Todd Snyder. It was Simmons' turn to take the pole at a record speed of 109.342 mph, and take the win. While Snyder was credited with second place, he was a substantial 2.074 seconds behind at the checker. Simmons' third victory of the year established him as a slight favorite for championship honors with two events remaining. He also set a new record race average speed at 102.240 mph. Townsend Bell was the surprise third place finisher. Sepp Koster matched his best early season results with a fourth place finish. Thomas Schie recovered from an unhappy Laguna Seca outing to take the last slot in the top five. The Simmons-Snyder championship matchup will have some interesting permutations, in that Barber Dodge rules allow only the ten top finishers to count.

Barber Dodge Pro Series Race 11
Homestead Motorsports Complex
Homestead, FL
October 17, 1998
22 Laps, 40:07 Minutes

NILTON ROSSONI ROARS BACK IN ACTION WITH HOMESTEAD VICTORY

After missing the two previous rounds, Nilton Rossoni matched his Road America win with victory at Homestead. Alex Gurney of California's racing Gurney family, claimed his first pole of the year, at 94.123 mph, a record. He led the first three laps, the rest was all Rossoni. The Brazilian was a comfortable 3.462 seconds ahead of runner-up Jeff Simmons at the checkered flag. Just astern of Simmons was his title rival Todd Snyder. Even the two point differential between second and third place could be critical with only the return visit to Laguna Seca remaining on the schedule. Polesitter Gurney salvaged fourth place, his best finish of the year. Last of the top five was Thomas Schie. With Rossoni performing so ably in his last two outings, its natural to speculate what he might have been able to do without missing three events.

Barber Dodge Pro Series Race 12
Laguna Seca Raceway
Monterey, CA
October 25, 1998
25 Laps, 41:01 Minutes

TODD SNYDER SCORES IN LAGUNA SECA FINALE. JEFF SIMMONS TAKES THE TITLE.

Todd Snyder met the challenge head on. He had to win the season ending race at Laguna Seca to have any realistic chance at the title. He did, shuffling polesitter Will Langhorne aside on the first lap and leading every subsequent lap to the checker. What he couldn't do was keep points leader Jeff Simmons out of second place, and the 16 points that go with it. Final score Simmons 158, Snyder 155. After a season long struggle, the title and its $300,000 went to Simmons. Langhorne faded to seventh at the end. Nilton Rossoni finished with a fine third place. Samer Hindi notched fifth place. Thomas Schie was scored in last place today but earned third place for the season with 114 points. Tenth today, Giovanni Anapoli was the year's fourth place finisher at 103. Langhorne was the final driver in the year's top five at 98 points.

Added Incentive... Barber Dodge Pro Series drivers competed for a record $1.1 million in prize money in 1998.

Worthy Champion... **Jeff Simmons** ran off three victories from the pole, took a hotly contested title race despite missing the first event. (158 Barber Dodge points)

Sidell Tilghman

2&3 Three race winner **Todd Snyder** (left) took the season's opening event, its finale, and one race in between, still came up three points short of the title. (155 Barber Dodge points) Twice victorious **Thomas Schie** (right) also scored a single pole enroute to third place in the championship. (114 Barber Dodge points)

Sidell Tilghman

4 Consistency Counts... **Giovanni Anapoli** didn't make it to the winner's circle, but was rarely out of the points. (103 Barber Dodge points)

Richard Dole

5 Grand Rapids Winner... **Will Langhorne** was brilliant on occasions, but failed to garner points in three races. (98 Barber Dodge points)

Sidell Tilghman

6 Brilliant Brazilian... **Nilton Rossoni** started only eight of the 12 events, had two wins and a third in his last three. (83 Barber Dodge points)

NTB TRANS-AM TOUR
Paul Gentilozzi Rockets to the Trans-Am Title

Ken Hawking

Going into the 1998 NTB Trans-Am Tour, Paul Gentilozzi's Rocketsports team had all the chips, the best cars, spanking new Corvettes, the most experienced crew, and the best driver, himself. He played the chips well and claimed the title handily, winning more than half of the 13 races in the Tour. Though commanding, Gentilozzi's performance failed to match the run-away of the 1997 titleist, Tommy Kendall of Roush Racing fame, a four time champion. Both Roush and Kendall bowed out of Trans-Am at the end of '97. So good was the Rocketsports organization that 51 year old teammate Bill Saunders, never before a winner on the Trans-Am Tour, won two races in a row, Cleveland and West Michigan, and was the runner-up part of a one-two finish for Rocketsports at Mid-Ohio. Between the pair, they led 469 of the year's 674 laps. Gentilozzi was the fastest qualifier in nine of the 13 events. Gentilozzi's closest competitor all year was Brian Simo in the Valvoline Mustang who revived an old and heated rivalry. Simo finally won his first Trans-Am race at Pikes Peak and followed it up with the win at Houston in the series finale. Simo also picked up a pair of pole positions and harassed Gentilozzi all season enroute to the runner-up slot in the championship (292 points) compared to Gentilozzi's winning

tally of 342. Saunders, in the second AutoLink Corvette, came close to making it a Rocketsports one-two in the title chase but had to settle for third place at season end, his best showing, with 283 points.

Rookie of the Year Chris Neville was the top Camaro driver, fast and consistent all year; he completed 670 of the 674 total laps of competition, failed to make the top ten only once all year. He showed maturity rare for a newcomer and a turn of speed that marks him as a serious contender for top honors in 1999; fourth place in the Tour (281 points).

Most Improved Driver John W. Miller IV, also Camaro mounted, started off the season with a display of speed that had him tagged as a real threat to points leader Gentilozzi. He qualified on the front row at the Long Beach opener, finished a solid third, and followed up with another third. At LIme Rock and Mid-Ohio he was again in a front row starting position, finished just short of the podium. His season's highpoint was a well earned second place at Minnesota. His second half was less productive, but still good enough for 263 points and fifth place in the year's standings.

Mustang man Ross Thompson was the first rookie of the year to make the podium, with a third at Lime Rock. Late in the season he scored a fine second place at Pikes

Peak. In between he occasionally exhibited overenthusiasm which can be costly. Nonetheless he chalked up 240 points and sixth place for the year.

Veteran Leighton Reese, a Pontiac Grand Prix exponent, managed a career best second place at Detroit, coming from tenth at the start. That and a pair of third places contributed to his season total of 207, seventh best of the year. Oldest rookie, at 40, Bruce Qvale comes from a well known West Coast road racing family. Up from the SCCA amateur ranks, the Mustang driver adapted quickly to the Trans-Am Tour. He was a runner-up twice and third once. At 203 points he was eighth for the year and the third highest placed rookie. Michael Lewis, also at the wheel of a Mustang, gained top qualifying honors at Cleveland, finished third. He was the runner-up in the mixed-up Lime Rock outing and picked up another third place at Minnesota. Ninth place (195 points) was less than had been expected of him at the beginning of the year.

Randy Ruhlman, driving a Mustang, made the "Fast Five" qualifying group three times and finished in the top five three times. Other times mechanical problems prevented him from displaying his true ability. He was the tenth member of the year's "Top Ten" club.

Trans-Am Titan... **Paul Gentilozzi** put his stamp on the 1998 NTB Trans-Am Tour; most wins (7), most poles (9), most laps led (469 of 674), and most points (342 NTB Trans-Am points).

Dan Bianchi

2 Hot Pursuer... **Brian Simo** continued his long term heated rivalry with Gentilozzi, scored two victories, his first in Trans-Am, plus two poles for runner-up honors. (292 NTB Trans-Am points)

3 Gentilozzi Teammate... **Bill Saunders** held up Rocketsports Racing's honors with two wins, first in his career, on the occasions when the team leader had an off day. (283 NTB Trans-Am points).

Dan Bianchi

4 Rookie of the Year... **Chris Neville** failed to complete only four of the year's 674 laps, failed to make the top ten only once. (281 NTB Trans-Am points)

5 Most Improved Driver... **John W. Miller IV** had a pair of podium appearances in the year's first two races, plus a second at Minnesota. His second half season was less productive. (263 NTB Trans-Am points)

Dan Bianchi

6 Rapid Rookie... **Ross Thompson** collected third place at Lime Rock, second at Pikes Peak. In between he was occasionally a victim of overenthusiasm. (240 NTB Trans-Am points)

Dan Bianchi

7 Pontiac Pilot... **Leighton Reese** managed a career best second place in Detroit, the most hotly contested event on the Tour. (207 NTB Trans-Am points)

8 Quick Learner... **Bruce Qvale**, up from the amateur ranks, in a Mustang, scored a pair of runner-up finishes and a third place in his freshman year on the Tour. (203 NTB Trans-Am points)

10 Stung by Mechanical Problems... **Randy Ruhlman** failed to make a podium but exhibited good speed when preparation of his Mustang allowed. (194 NTB Trans-Am points)

Ken Hawking

9 Fast Qualifier... **Michael Lewis**, in a Mustang, was the only driver other than Gentilozzi and Simo to gain a pole position (Cleveland). His best finish was a second at Lime Rock. (195 NTB Trans-Am points)

NTB Trans-Am Tour Race 1
Long Beach Street Course
Long Beach, CA
April 5, 1998
52 Laps, 83 Miles

PAUL GENTILOZZI BREEZES TO VICTORY IN LONG BEACH OPENER

Paul Gentilozzi's seasoned Rocket-sports crew had done their homework well. His new Corvette was well tested, groomed to perfection. All he had to do was drive it. Drive it Gentilozzi did. He claimed the pole, got away in front at the start and showed his tailpipes to the field for the full 52 laps. Eased up, he was 6.536 seconds in front of endurance specialist Stu Hayner in a Camaro at the finish. Sophomore driver John W. Miller IV got his season off to a solid start with third place, despite fading brakes toward the end of the race. Chris Neville, in his first Trans-Am outing, placed fourth, indicating a good grasp of the fine points of the

Tour. Gentilozzi teammate Bill Saunders claimed fifth place, after losing in a duel with Neville. The driver expected to give Gentilozzi the most competition over the season, Brian Simo, failed to be a factor. Qualifying was limited to a short period on Sunday due to wet track conditions on Saturday and Simo's qualifying effort wasn't good enough to make him an immediate front runner. He'll be heard from as the season develops.

NTB Trans-Am Tour Race 2
Homestead Motorsports Complex
Homestead, FL
May 17, 1998
45 Laps, 100 Miles

PAUL GENTILOZZI BESTS BRIAN SIMO FOR THE HOMESTEAD VICTORY

It was shaping up as one of those ding dong Paul Gentilozzi-Brian Simo battles of seasons past, but on lap 34 Gentilozzi put Simo away for the last time and ran off with the victory. Gentilozzi was on the pole, but Simo grabbed the lead on lap three. Gentilozzi grabbed it back 15 laps later. Simo then got by for five tours out front. But Gentilozzi was not to be denied. He made the race's final pass for the lead and pulled away to a solid .587 second cushion over Simo at the finish. No flying fiberglass body parts this time, Gentilozzi had a clear-cut edge. Nobody else got close, but John W. Miller IV, showing newfound speed this year, was the class of the other 34 starters, finishing third. Veteran Randy Ruhlman had the best finish of his Trans-Am career, fourth. Rookie Chris Neville got his Trans-Am career off to a workmanlike start with a solid fifth place. Gentilozzi teammate Bill Saunders got involved in a tangle and finished 12th. With his second win in a row Gentilozzi is serving notice that he intends to keep the pressure on in his campaign for the title.

NTB Trans-Am Tour Race 3
Lime Rock Park
Lakeville, CT
May 25, 1998
66 Laps, 100 Miles

LOU GIGLIOTTI WINS A WET AND CONFUSED LIME ROCK RACE

Protests were flying faster than the pace car at the conclusion of a wet and wild Dodge Dealers Grand Prix at Lime Rock Park. All the protests however, were shot down and the driver over the finish line first, Lou Gigliotti, was confirmed as the official winner. It was his first trip to victory circle. How he got there is a tangled tale. The race started in the rain under yellow with first time pole-sitter Brian Simo getting passed by John W. Miller IV when the green came out because Simo's inside lane had more water. Simo got the lead back, lost it when he went off course and grazed two cars parked in the grass. He got back on in third place behind Miller and Paul Gentilozzi. After getting the one lap to go sign, Gigliotti slammed into Simo, cutting his own tire but still getting past both

Simo and Gentilozzi. In the ensuing confusion Simo regained first place only to go into the tire barrier two laps later. Gigliotti meanwhile made not one, but two, stops for tires. When the green resumed, Gentilozzi, in the lead, took off followed by Bill Saunders, Miller, Neville, and Lewis. The officials then ruled that the top four had passed the pace car. They were brought in and held until they were down a lap. Guess who is now in the lead? None other than Gigliotti who had put on slicks because he didn't have any more rain tires. Michael Lewis, Ross Thompson, Don Sak, and John Halbing completed the top five. Gentilozzi finished seventh and was not amused. His protest was disallowed.

NTB Trans-Am Tour Race 4
Raceway on Belle Isle Park
Detroit, MI
June 6, 1998
42 Laps, 100 Miles

GENTILOZZI DOMINATES DETROIT'S MOTOR CITY 100

Detroit's Motor City 100, played out before a knowledgeable crowd of automotive executives and enthusiasts, is the one Trans-Am race drivers want most to win. Paul Gentilozzi, in the no. 3 AutoLink Corvette, wanted the win more than any of the other 32 starters and had the equipment to capitalize on his desires. He had been trying for ten years to prevail in Detroit without success and called his victory,"the most satisfying thing I'll ever do in motorsports." Gentilozzi started on the pole, pulled out a handsome lead. He was never truly pressed along the way to a front running victory that gave him a 1.976 second margin over runner-up Leighton Reese at the checker. Just to complete a statistical hat trick, he set the race's fastest lap. Gentilozzi teammate Bill Saunders held down second place at the start but was bumped by Ross Thompson. He managed to recover but fell victim to engine problems after 30 laps. Brian Simo made several valiant attempts to get by Saunders in the early going but succeeded only in spinning and was fortunate to salvage fifth place. Rookie Bruce Qvale took down third place, with fourth going to Rick Dittman.

Soggy Surprise... Lou Gigliotti Tops the Field at Lime Rock

Nigel Kinrade

NTB Trans-Am Tour Race 5	NTB Trans-Am Tour Race 6	NTB Trans-Am Tour Race 7
Mid-Ohio Sports Car Course	Minneapolis Street Course	Burke Lakefront Airport
Lexington, OH	Minneapolis, MN	Cleveland, OH
June 14, 1998	June 28, 1998	July 11, 1998
45 Laps, 100 Miles	63 Laps, 100 Miles	42 Laps, 90 Miles

PAUL GENTILOZZI MAKES IT TWO IN A ROW AT MID-OHIO

PAUL GENTILOZZI MASTERS MINNEAPOLIS' STREET CIRCUIT

BILL SAUNDERS STEPS IN FOR THE CLEVELAND WIN

Paul Gentilozzi, again the polesitter, had the Mid-Ohio race so well in hand that he could, and did, afford to let teammate Bill Saunders borrow the lead for seven tours, starting with lap 30. With eight laps to go Gentilozzi, in his AutoLink Corvette, again took over the leader's mantle kept it all the way to the checker. He left the scene with 156 points, a sizeable bulge over second place John W. Miller IV who finished fourth today. Brian Simo had a typically aggressive day, but by the closing stages had used up his tires and could do no better than third. Rookie Bruce Qvale, in his Ford Mustang Cobra, had another worthwhile outing good for fifth place.

As a measure of Gentilozzi's superiority today, he, at one point, had a five second edge over the second place runner, Saunders.

Most of the Trans-Am Tour drivers on Minneapolis' grueling street circuit were happy to see the yellow flag fly four laps from the end. Not Paul Gentilozzi. He had a 20 second lead and was still full of fight. "I had a lot of car left. I was looking forward to a good finish." Brian Simo was hounding Gentilozzi, the polesitter, in the early going, but on lap eight brake problems helped put him into the tire barrier. He bulled his way out, and recovered to finish fifth, albeit with highly altered bodywork. With Simo demoted, John W. Miller IV took over second place, which he held to the end, without making any meaningful move on Gentilozzi. Michael Lewis held off Bill Saunders for third. Rookie Bruce Qvale had an exciting day, moving all the way from 24th at the start to fourth, only to be betrayed by a broken axle on lap 47.

When Paul Gentilozzi's engine failed while he was leading on lap 36, teammate Bill Saunders stepped into the breach. He pressured leader Brian Simo for three hotly contested laps, before edging into the lead on lap 36 with three more circuits to go. Simo and Gentilozzi had been putting on one of their crowd pleasing tussles for virtually the entire race until Gentilozzi's untimely departure, often swapping the lead several times in a single lap. Saunders was ecstatic at the win, his first ever, particularly since he bested Simo. For a change, Gentilozzi wasn't on the pole. Chris Lewis, a 23 year veteran was, for the first time in his career. His third place finish in the race made the day doubly enjoyable. Chris Neville took down fourth in the finishing order, with fifth going to veteran Randy Ruhlman.

NTB Trans-Am Tour Race 8
Grand Rapids Street Course
Grand Rapids, MI
July 26, 1998
64 Laps, 100 Miles

BILL SAUNDERS STREAKS TO TWO IN A ROW AT GRAND RAPIDS

Elevated into the limelight of victory circle by Paul Gentilozzi's blown engine last time out, nobody expected Bill Saunders to win the next outing as well. But win he did after polesitter Gentilozzi's hood blew off during one of his hammer and tong battles with Brian Simo. Simo then used up his tires staying ahead of an aerodynamically wounded but still feisty Gentilozzi. This set the stage for Saunders to move into the lead over Simo and build up a husky 44.867 second margin of victory over Bruce Qvale at the finish. Qvale and Chris Neville both got past Simo, who was forced to nurse worn tires.

Simo did manage to salvage fourth place ahead of Leighton Reese in fifth. Gentilozzi limped home in sixth place, better than the 33rd of his last outing. At age 51 and with 70 Trans-Am starts in his log book, Saunders is having the kind of banner year, with two victories and eight races to go, he could only have dreamed of prior to the start of his Rocketsports year.

NTB Trans-Am Tour Race 9
Trois-Rivieres Street Course
Trois-Rivieres, Canada
August 2, 1998
55 Laps, 85 Miles

PAUL GENTILOZZI GETS BACK ON TOP AT TROIS-RIVIERES

Never noted for hanging back when he had the horsepower to be in front, Paul Gentilozzi, on the pole again, did just that at Trois-Rivieres. In a tire conservation strate-

gy that worked to perfection, he let arch rival Brian Simo, along with Gentilozzi teammate Bill Saunders jump into the lead at the start. Simo's all out approach, which involved a pit stop for tires might have worked except that mechanical failure struck after 22 laps, putting him on the sidelines. Gentilozzi took over the lead on the Simo stop and ran off the remaining 44 laps without incident, building up a 30.844 second cushion over rapid rookie Bruce Qvale, who gained his second runner-up slot in a row. Saunders, too, had to pit for tires, dropping him to seventh at the checker. Another promising rookie, Chris Neville, claimed third place despite a stop-and-go penalty for passing under yellow. John W. Miller IV and Michael Lewis completed the top five. Max Lagod at one stage appeared to have a chance of catching Gentilozzi, but a cut tire and an off-song motor put him on the sidelines.

Stu Hayner Slips By Bill Saunders for the Road America Win

NTB Trans-Am Tour Race 10
Watkins Glen International
Watkins Glen, NY
August 8, 1998
42 Laps, 100 Miles

WATKINS GLEN GOES TO PAUL GENTILOZZI

Paul Gentilozzi scored his seventh victory of the season, running off every lap in front of the field from the pole, his ninth of the year. What he didn't score was his tenth fastest lap of the year. That honor went to Stu Hayner at 120.261 mph on the last lap. Though Gentilozzi won, Hayner might well have challenged him had the race gone another five laps. Hayner qualified fourth fastest but was forced to start 42nd due to lateness in presenting his race car for pre-race inspection. His charge through the huge field, the largest in recent history, captured the crowd's affection even though it fell just short. He was right on the heels of runner-

up Brian Simo, who was 1.935 seconds behind Gentilozzi when the checker waved. Chris Neville and John W. Miller IV rounded out the top five. Another runner who made huge strides towards the front during the race was Bill Saunders, who started 41st and finished sixth. His fine run however, lacked the élan provided by Hayner's dash. "I really think we had the best car on the track at the end," said an exhilarated Hayner.

NTB Trans-Am Tour Race 11
Road America
Elkhart Lake, WI
August 15, 1998
25 Laps, 100 Miles

STU HAYNER AMBUSHES BILL SAUNDERS FOR ROAD AMERICA VICTORY

At the start of the last lap at Road America it looked like another one-two Rocketsports rout with Paul Gentilozzi comfortably out front and

Bill Saunders riding shotgun. Arch rival Brian Simo was in the picture but had used up his car fighting Gentilozzi, again the polesitter, for the lead. Stu Hayner, who had qualified fourth, was a distant fourth. Things changed rapidly. Gentilozzi dropped to the wayside, Simo faded, and a charging Hayner caught Saunders napping and swept by into an uncontested lead. By the time Saunders was aware of Hayner it was all over. Hayner had his first Trans-Am win in only 12 starts. A downcast Saunders could only state, "I didn't know he was coming. I just let him by." Chris Neville scored another third place, useful in his quest for Rookie of the Year honors. Lou Gigliotti, in a new Corvette, finished fourth ahead of John W. Miller IV. A hero at Cleveland and Grand Rapids after Gentilozzi had troubles, Saunders could have played the White Knight role for Rocketsports again, but missed the opportunity.

NTB Trans-Am Tour Race 12
Pikes Peak International Raceway
Fountain, CO
September 27, 1998
75 Laps, 98 Miles

BRIAN SIMO BREAKS THROUGH FOR VICTORY AT PIKES PEAK

PAUL GENTILOZZI TAKES THE TITLE

Right from the early rounds of the 1998 NTB Trans-Am Tour, two happenings seemed inevitable; Paul Gentilozzi would corral his first championship, Brian Simo, often close but never a winner, would take his first trip to victory circle. Simo's victory, coming on his 60th Trans-Am start, was clear-cut and conclusive. He started on the pole, led every lap in his Mustang, had a comfortable 2.485 second lead over Ross Thompson at the finish. This time there was no Paul Gentilozzi up front to pressure Simo into using up his car or his tires. Gentilozzi, suffering from the SCCA mandated reduction in his Corvette's spoiler, didn't even make the "Fast Five" qualifiers. He didn't make the top five at the finish either, but his seventh place was good enough to cinch his first Trans-Am championship. While there were celebrations in both camps, Simo's was the more exuberant, coming on top of a dominant victory. Gentilozzi, however, deserves full marks for his championship, well planned, well executed, well driven. Mustang driver Ross Thompson, the surprise second fastest qualifier, stayed fast all day, earned runner-up honors. Leighton Reese, Chris Neville, and Randy Ruhlman filled the other three places in the "Top Five."

NTB Trans-Am Tour Race 13
Houston Street Course
Houston, TX
October 3, 1998
60 Laps, 92 Miles

HOUSTON IS HOT, BRIAN SIMO HOTTER IN SECOND WIN IN A ROW

Paul Gentilozzi recovered from an off-form Pikes Peak performance to claim the pole at Houston and battle arch rival Brian Simo almost down to the wire. This time Simo came out on top, unlike many episodes in the past. Gentilozzi led the first 37 laps then let Simo by, hoping he'd self destruct. Simo charged off into a handsome lead, however, while preserving both his car and his tires. When the front running pair arrived on Stu Hayner's bumper to lap him they were frustrated. Simo managed to squeeze by on lap 54. Gentilozzi had a tougher time getting by Hayner and was delayed. The delay may have prompted him to overcook a passing attempt on Simo that landed him in the tire barrier. The miscue also allowed his teammate Bill Saunders to move into second place. Gentilozzi nursed his injured Corvette into third. Thus the season ending podium fittingly consisted of the three top points producers, though not in order. Simo took second in the title chase after champion Gentilozzi, with Saunders a worthy third. In today's action Ross Thompson was fourth with Michael Lewis fifth. It was a fitting end to an improved Trans-Am season that saw more entries, more prize money, and closer competition.

Well Launched... the Rocketsports Racing pair, champion Paul Gentilozzi, right, and third place Bill Saunders, left, were on a higher trajectory than their opposition. They had the most aerodynamically efficient cars, new Corvettes, the most experienced team, did the most testing of new Goodrich tires on proven BBS wheels. The results showed in Gentilozzi's seven wins and nine poles in 13 races and Saunders' two victories, his first ever.

Dan Bianchi

New for '99 American Le Mans Series
will feature Le Mans prototypes like the BMW V12 LMR (above) entered for Sebring. Also expected,
the factory Audi R8R and a Formula One Judd powered Riley & Scott private entry.